# Edexcel GCSE (9–1)

# Drama

Melissa Jones   Phil Cleaves

ALWAYS LEARNING

**PEARSON**

Published by Pearson Education Limited, 80 Strand, London, WC2R 0RL.

www.pearsonschoolsandfecolleges.co.uk

Copies of official specifications for all Edexcel qualifications may be found on the website: www.edexcel.com

Text © Pearson Education Limited 2016
Typeset by Tek-Art
Produced by Hart McLeod Ltd
Picture research by Alison Prior
Cover photo/illustration © Bridgeman Art Library/Private Collection

The rights of Melissa Jones and Phil Cleaves to be identified as authors of this work have been asserted by them in accordance with the Copyright, Designs and Patents Act 1988.

First published 2016

19 18 17 16
10 9 8 7 6 5 4 3 2 1

**British Library Cataloguing in Publication Data**
A catalogue record for this book is available from the British Library

ISBN 978 1 292 15068 0

Printed in Slovakia by Neografia

**Acknowledgements**
We are grateful to the following for permission to reproduce copyright material:

**Text**
Extract on page 20 from *An Inspector Calls*, Heinemann Plays for 14-16+ (J.B. Priestley); Extract on page 29 from *The Crucible*, Student Edition, Methuen Drama (Arthur Miller). Reprinted with permission of Wylie UK; Extract on page 37 from *The Government Inspector*, Faber & Faber (Nikolai Gogol adapted by David Harrower); Extract on page 44 from *New Longman Shakespeare. Twelfth Night*, Pearson Education Limited (William Shakespeare (Author), John O'Connor (Editor)); Extract on page 50 from *DNA*, School Edition (Dennis Kelly 2009), © Dennis Kelly 2008. By kind permission of Oberon Books Ltd.; Extract on page 57 from *1984 (Nineteen Eighty-Four) (Oberon Modern Plays)*, Oberon Books (Duncan Macmillan, George Orwell, Robert Icke 2013); Stage adaptation © Robert Icke and Duncan Macmillan 2013. By kind permission of Oberon Books Ltd.; Extract on page 57 from *1984 (Nineteen Eighty-Four) (Oberon Modern Plays)*, Headlong Education Pack, Oberon (George Orwell, Duncan Macmillan, Robert Icke 2013); Stage adaptation © Robert Icke and Duncan Macmillan 2013. By kind permission of Oberon Books Ltd.; Extract on page 57 adapted from *Nineteen Eighty-Four by George Orwell* (Copyright © George Orwell, 1948), reprinted by permission of Bill Hamilton as the Literary Executor of the Estate of the Late Sonia Brownell Orwell; Quote on page 61 from http://www.thedoublenegative.co.uk/2013/11/1984-reviewed/, The Double Negative, reprinted with kind permission of The Double Negative (www.thedoublenegative.co.uk); Extract on page 64 from *Blue Stockings (NHB Modern Plays)*, Nick Hern Books (Jessica Swale), Excerpts from BLUE STOCKINGS copyright © Jessica Swale 2013, reprinted with permission from Nick Hern Books: www.nickhernbooks.co.uk; Extract

on page 71 from *Dr Korczak's Example* (David Greig); Extract on page 114 from *Lord of the Flies: Acting Edition: Play*, Acting edition, Faber & Faber (William Golding, Nigel Williams (Adapter)).

The author and publisher would like to thank the following individuals and organisations for permission to reproduce photographs:

(Key: b-bottom; c-centre; l-left; r-right; t-top)

**Alamy Images:** Eddie Gerald 71, George Leroy 14, Israel Images 73, PF-(bygone1) 64; **Bridgeman Art Library Ltd:** Peabody Essex Museum, Salem / Massachusetts / Bridgeman 29; **Colin Winslow:** 49b; **Graham Michael Production Photography (c) Graham Michael 2008:** Graham Michael 35; **Hull Truck Theatre:** 55r; **Mike Lees:** 28; **Photostage Ltd:** 00076304 62, Donald Cooper 9, 21, 45, 49tr; **Robert Workman:** 55l; **Science Photo Library Ltd:** Jim Amos 18; **Simon Annand:** 51; **TopFoto:** Ivan Kynd 8, Johan Perrson / ArenaPAL 19, Johan Persson / ArenaPAL 98, 107, 111, 114, Johan Persson / ArenaPAL 98, 107, 111, 114, Marilyn Kingwall / ArenaPAL 97, Marilyn Kingwill / ArenaPAL 61, Nigel Norrington 42, Nigel Norrington / ArenaPAL 47, 70l, 70r, Nigel Norrington / ArenaPAL 47, 70l, 70r, Nigel Norrington / ArenaPAL 47, 70l, 70r, Nigel NorringtonArenaPAL 65, Nobby Clarke 38, Sophie Baker / ArenaPAL 12; **Unicorn Theatre:** 74; **York Theatre Royal:** Set Designed by Dawn Allsopp, Costumes Designed by Catherine Chapman, Directed by Juliet Forster, Photography by Karl Andre 34

**Cover images:** *Front:* **Bridgeman Art Library Ltd:** Front cover of the music score for 'Tom Foolery Lancers', by H. L. D'Arcy Jaxone, 1898 (colour litho), Banks, H. G. (19th century) / Private Collection

All other images © Pearson Education

**Websites**
Pearson Education Limited is not responsible for the content of any external internet sites. It is essential for tutors to preview each website before using it in class so as to ensure that the URL is still accurate, relevant and appropriate. We suggest that tutors bookmark useful websites and consider enabling students to access them through the school/college intranet.

**A note from the publisher**
In order to ensure that this resource offers high-quality support for the associated Pearson qualification, it has been through a review process by the awarding body. This process confirms that this resource fully covers the teaching and learning content of the specification or part of a specification at which it is aimed. It also confirms that it demonstrates an appropriate balance between the development of subject skills, knowledge and understanding, in addition to preparation for assessment.

Endorsement does not cover any guidance on assessment activities or processes (e.g. practice questions or advice on how to answer assessment questions), included in the resource nor does it prescribe any particular approach to the teaching or delivery of a related course.

While the publishers have made every attempt to ensure that advice on the qualification and its assessment is accurate, the official specification and associated assessment guidance materials are the only authoritative source of information and should always be referred to for definitive guidance.

Pearson examiners have not contributed to any sections in this resource relevant to examination papers for which they have responsibility.

Examiners will not use endorsed resources as a source of material for any assessment set by Pearson.

Endorsement of a resource does not mean that the resource is required to achieve this Pearson qualification, nor does it mean that it is the only suitable material available to support the qualification, and any resource lists produced by the awarding body shall include this and other appropriate resources.

# Contents

# Foreword

**You can kill the King without a sword, and you can light the fire without a match. What needs to burn is your imagination.**

*Stanislavki (An Actor Prepares)*

Think back a long, long way. Before TV, iPhones, Facebook. Way back, when we'd only just left caves, when we still tore meat from the bone and chased beasts through the forest. Early man, returning from the hunt, would gather together, perform rituals and tell stories.

We would *tell stories*. Storytelling is almost as old as the human race.

As soon as we could talk, we told tales. And before long, we were standing up and acting them out. The world's oldest theatre, in Epidaurus, is over two thousand years old. Think about it. Which other forms of entertainment have such staying power, and such universal appeal? Because not only is theatre one of the oldest human activities, but it's universal. It exists in every culture of the world, from Indian Kathakali to Japanese Noh theatre. So the question is- why? Why, in an era of smart phones and 3D printers, do we still choose to spend time watching plays, as our toga-wearing ancestors did in Ancient Greece?

Perhaps it is because it is magic. It's escapism. In the theatre, we can put aside the troubles of daily life and imagine ourselves somewhere else entirely; in Illyria watching a love story unfurl, in Newcastle, watching a boy sneak secretly to ballet class …

Perhaps it's because we're curious. Theatre allows us to experience a life beyond our life, to explore the world, to be nosey, to be royalty, to go to a ball in Regency Bath, to experience love, ambition, hatred, grief, the fear of being accused of witchcraft, the joy of discovering your twin is still alive, without the pain of the real experience.

Perhaps it's because it helps us understand. Theatre puts us firmly in someone else's shoes; to see the world through the eyes of an autistic kid, to feel the weight of expectation on a stammering King, to experience the frustrations of life as a female scientist. Theatre teaches us empathy. It teaches us not to judge.

The list goes on. Theatre allows us to question, to listen, to feel, to learn. By its very nature as a mirror to life, it reflects an enormous landscape of experiences. And if we're to do justice to the plays we want to perform – or to create – then we must explore these worlds in detail. For me, that research is one of the most fascinating aspects of the job. In my career as a playwright and director I've tested the waters in Bath for *The Rivals,* I've helped with the lambing for *Far from the Madding Crowd,* I've visited psychiatric wards for *Bedlam,* I've been caught up in protests writing *Blue Stockings,* I've interviewed genocide survivors for *The Overwhelming.* I even learnt to make pork pies for *Andersen's English.* Few other careers could offer quite such a varied working day.

But for me, there's one aspect of theatre which transcends all others. And that's theatre's capacity to bring joy. It allows us to laugh, to feel, to embrace life wholeheartedly. For me, that joy comes as much from making work as it does from watching plays. I love to work with actors. I love to share a rehearsal room with a group of creative people, to begin on Monday with scraps of paper and finish on Friday with a draft. I love to throw ideas around with composers, then listen as the band transforms my scrappy lyrics into a song I'll be singing all the way home. And I love the ensemble. The fact that we're a team. We make something together. Something that didn't exist before and now, through all our efforts, it does.

You are so lucky, embarking on this course. There has never been a more exciting time to get started in the theatre. You have everything from the simple word to the most cutting edge technology to play with. The scope for invention is unparalleled.

It won't be easy. Making theatre requires torrents of hard graft; not just creativity, but the architecture of forming a story, the mathematics of production, the determination to succeed, the drafting and redrafting, the rehearsals, the technical demands, the pressure. But when has anything easy ever been worthwhile? What are you waiting for? Stop reading and go and make some theatre.

I wish you all the luck in the world.

Enjoy the magic.

Jessica Swale

# Introduction

Welcome to GCSE Drama. There will be many reasons why you have chosen to take Drama. No doubt they will be rooted in practical work and collaboration. Practical exploration is central to this course, with opportunities to be a deviser, a performer, a designer and an active audience member. You will be challenged to:

* develop your creative skills
* work as part of a team to achieve exciting and engaging performances
* develop your analysis and evaluation skills.

GCSE Drama will give you the confidence to:

* work collaboratively
* communicate with clarity and creativity.

This book will focus on how to approach the analysis and evaluation of your own work and the work of others in preparation for the written exam in component 3. It is important to appreciate that the knowledge and understanding you develop during work on all components will prepare you for your final written exam, however, so understanding how the whole course fits together will help you to get the most out of each component.

## GCSE (9–1) Drama overview

### Component 1: Devising

#### 40% of GCSE – 60 marks

As a performer or a designer you will work in a group to create and develop an original piece of drama in response to a stimulus.

The performance or design realisation of your devised drama is worth 15 marks.

The analysis and evaluation of both development and performance will be presented as a written or recorded/verbal portfolio worth 45 marks.

### Component 2: Performance from text

#### 20% of GCSE – 48 marks

As a performer or a designer you will explore two key extracts from a performance text. You will then create a performance of the two key extracts and present it to a visiting examiner. The performance or design of each key extract is worth 24 marks.

### Component 3: Theatre makers in practice

#### 40% of GCSE – 60 marks

1 hour 30 minutes, written exam

#### Section A Bringing texts to life – 45 marks

This section will ask you to demonstrate knowledge and understanding of how a performance text can be developed and performed. The performance text will be chosen by your teacher and you will practically explore the whole text in preparation for the exam. You will not be able to take your text into the exam, but you will be given an extract from the text to help you respond to the questions.

#### Section B Live theatre evaluation – 15 marks

This section will ask you to analyse and evaluate a live theatre performance that you have seen during the course. You are allowed to bring 500 words of notes into the exam to help you respond to the questions.

# Overview GCSE (9–1) Drama

## Component 1 Devising

You will collaborate with a group to create a new and original performance in response to a stimulus. You can choose to be assessed as a performer or a designer. Use the following checklists to help you.

### AO1 Create and develop ideas to communicate meaning for theatrical performance (30 marks)

The process must be active and practical. You must keep a record of your contribution to help you evidence your work in the portfolio.

- [ ] Choose and research a stimulus: understand the social, historical and cultural contexts and surrounding issues.
- [ ] Establish the aims and objectives: what do you want your audience to experience?
- [ ] Practical exploration: improvisation; tableaux; movement and physical sequences; role and characterisation.
- [ ] Discover the genre, style and form.
- [ ] Develop the structure.

### AO2 Apply theatrical skills to realise artistic intentions in live performance (15 marks)

- [ ] Rehearse and learn lines.
- [ ] Collaborate with a group to adapt work in response to rehearsals.
- [ ] Use your voice: use of clarity, pace, inflection, pitch and projection.
- [ ] Use your physicality: use of space, gesture, stillness and stance.
- [ ] Combine vocal and physical skills.
- [ ] Develop a role and characterisation.
- [ ] Communicate with other performers and with the audience.
- [ ] Show an understanding of style, genre and theatrical conventions.
- [ ] Designers: costume, lighting, set or sound.

### AO4 Analyse and evaluate your own work and the work of others (15 marks)

You must present a written or recorded/verbal portfolio that responds to the following questions:

- [ ] What was your initial response to the stimuli and what were the intentions of the piece?
- [ ] What work did your group do in order to explore the stimuli and start to create ideas for performance?
- [ ] What were some of the significant moments during the development process and when rehearsing and refining your work?
- [ ] How did you consider genre, structure, character, form, style and language throughout the process?
- [ ] What health and safety issues did you have to consider?
- [ ] How effective was your contribution to the final performance?
- [ ] Were you successful in what you set out to achieve?

# Component 2 Performance from text

## AO2 Apply theatrical skills to realise artistic intentions in live performance (24 marks for each extract – 48 marks in total)

You will collaborate with a group to interpret a text. Then you will rehearse and refine two key extracts in preparation for a final performance. You will be assessed by an external examiner. Your teacher can help you to develop the piece. Use the following checklists to help you.

## Vocal and physical skills (performers)

☐ Understand how vocal choices of articulation, pitch, pace, pause, tone, inflection and volume support the meaning of the text.

☐ Develop control, variation and range of voice to support the meaning of the text.

☐ Understand how physical decisions about pace, size, flow, weight, control and orientation support the meaning of the text.

☐ Develop control, variation and range of spatial behaviour (proxemics), facial expression, gesture, gaze, posture, stillness, touch and bodily contact to support the meaning of the text.

## Characterisation and communication (performers)

☐ Understand the role and its context within the performance.

☐ Develop engaging characterisation with focus, confidence and commitment.

☐ Cultivate a sense of rapport with your fellow performers.

☐ Establish clear communication with the audience.

## Artistic intention and style/genre/theatrical conventions (performers and designers)

☐ Contribute fully to the realisation of the group's artistic intentions.

☐ Understand the style, genre and theatrical conventions.

☐ Support the presentation of the group's interpretation of the text in the performance/design realisation.

☐ Refine your performance so that it is dynamic, impactful and energetic (performers).

☐ Develop a design that enhances and enriches the overall production value (designers).

☐ Write 100–200 words for each extract explaining the intention of the performance/design.

## Design skills (designers)

☐ Understand how creative design choices communicate meaning with an audience.

☐ Develop visual/audio elements that are impactful and enhance mood, atmosphere and style.

☐ Use the time and resources available creatively.

☐ Understand how materials and production elements can be applied to complement the performance.

## Communication and contribution to performance as whole (designers)

☐ Understand how the design reflects its context and purpose within the performance.

☐ Develop connections between design choices and the content of the performance.

☐ Communicate and collaborate with performers to create a design that shows cohesion with the content of the performance.

# Overview GCSE (9–1) Drama

## Component 3 Theatre makers in practice

You will sit a 1 hour 30-minute exam at the end of your course. You will explore practically how a complete performance text might be interpreted and realised from 'page to stage'. You will also analyse and evaluate your experience of a live theatre performance as an informed member of the audience. Use drama-specific vocabulary and terminology in your writing. Use the following checklists to help you.

### Section A Bringing texts to life (45 marks)

#### AO3 Demonstrate knowledge and understanding of how drama and theatre is developed and performed

- [ ] Understand the performance text in enough depth to be able to respond to the extract in the exam without the use of your own full text.
- [ ] Understand how performers use acting style and purpose, including vocal and physical skills, to create impact and meaning.
- [ ] Understand how designers use set and props to create impact and meaning.
- [ ] Understand how designers use lighting and sound, including colour and music, to create impact and meaning.
- [ ] Understand how designers use costume and make-up to create impact and meaning.
- [ ] Understand how directors use the stage space and spatial relationships to create impact and meaning.
- [ ] Develop appropriate interpretations of the text from the perspective of performer, designer and director.
- [ ] Know how performers, directors and designers influence performance style, design elements and staging to communicate meaning to an audience.
- [ ] Understand the playwright's use of meaning, genre, structure, character, form, style, language and stage directions for communication between performer and audience.
- [ ] Develop vocal and physical interpretation of characters.
- [ ] Understand the performance style and theatrical conventions.
- [ ] Understand the practices used in 21st-century theatre-making.
- [ ] Know the social, historical, political and cultural context of the period in which the text was written and performed.

### Section B Live theatre evaluation (15 marks)

#### AO4 Analyse and evaluate their own work and the work of others

- [ ] Attend a live theatre production.
- [ ] Write a maximum of 500 words of notes that can be taken into the exam.
- [ ] Know the details of the title, venue and date seen.
- [ ] Know the names of performers and their specific roles.
- [ ] Know specific details about costume, set, lighting and sound.
- [ ] Know the director's name, their concept/interpretation and the style of performance.
- [ ] Know what type of theatre space was used: proscenium, traverse, in-the-round, etc.
- [ ] Understand how the performance created an impact on you as an individual and the audience as a whole.
- [ ] Understand how the key ideas and themes were communicated in the performance.

# Assessment objectives

| You must: | | % of GCSE |
|---|---|---|
| AO1 | Create and develop ideas to communicate meaning for theatrical performance | 20 |
| AO2 | Apply theatrical skills to realise artistic intentions in live performance | 30 |
| AO3 | Demonstrate knowledge and understanding of how drama and theatre is developed and performed | 30 |
| AO4 | Analyse and evaluate your own work and the work of others | 20 |
| **Total** | | **100** |

## Breakdown of assessment objectives

| Component | Assessment Objectives | | | | Total for all assessment objectives |
|---|---|---|---|---|---|
| | AO1 % | AO2 % | AO3 % | AO4 % | |
| Component 1: Devising | 20 | 10 | 0 | 10 | 40% |
| Component 2: Performance from text | 0 | 20 | 0 | 0 | 20% |
| Component 3: Theatre makers in practice | 0 | 0 | 30 | 10 | 40% |
| **Total for GCSE** | **20%** | **30%** | **30%** | **20%** | **100%** |

## Exam tip

Writing quickly and clearly is important in the exam. You should aim to practise the whole 1 hour 30-minute exam two or three times to ensure you are confident when splitting your time between questions. Practising under timed conditions will:

- help you to pace yourself
- allow you to improve and become more confident.

## Exam tip

The times in this example add up to 1 hour and 20 minutes. This saves you 10 minutes at the start of the exam to read the extract and all the questions.

## Exam tip

- Look out for the number of lines in the answer paper. This will indicate how much you should aim to write.
- Tackling the longer essay questions first can be a useful way to ensure you give appropriate time to the questions with the higher marks. Be careful to respond to the questions in the correct place in the answer booklet and make sure you answer all the questions!
- Remember that Q (b)(ii) will ask you to refer to the **whole play**. Make sure to reflect this in your answer.

# Exam skills: marks and timing

Your teacher will help you to prepare for the process of writing about practical drama in each section of the exam. This book is designed to support you and your teacher in getting ready for the examination.

Knowing what kinds of questions will be asked and how many marks each question will be worth will help you to organise your revision. The example below is one strategy for approaching the timing of the written exam. It is not the only approach to timing and you must carefully consider what is best for you. This strategy is based on the time being split evenly between each mark.

## Section A Bringing texts to life (45 marks)

Read the wording of the question carefully. Where a question asks for **two** ideas you must provide **two** points in order to maximise the marks awarded to your response. Similarly, where a question asks for **three** ideas you must provide **three** points in order to maximise the marks awarded to your response. The timings given are suggestions only to help you plan. Your teacher may also have some advice for how to approach timings.

### Question (a)(i) – 4 marks (6 minutes)

You must make **two** points about choices you would make as a performer. You must give an explanation of why you made each choice.

### Question (a)(ii) – 6 marks (8 minutes)

You must make **three** points about choices you would make as a performer. You must give a reason why you made each choice. Avoid repeating points in (a)(i) and (a)(ii).

### Question (b)(i) – 9 marks (12 minutes)

This requires a longer 'essay-style' response. You should focus your argument around one element.

### Question (b)(ii) – 12 marks (16 minutes)

This requires a longer 'essay-style' response. You will be given **three** areas in the question that you must refer to in your response. Split your essay evenly across the **three** areas.

### Question (c) – 14 marks (18 minutes)

This requires a longer 'essay-style' response. This question will want you to give a detailed discussion of **one** element of your production of this extract.

## Section B: Live Theatre Evaluation – 15 marks

### Question 9 (a) – 6 marks (8 minutes)

This requires a short 'essay style' response.

### Question 9 (b) – 9 marks (12 minutes)

This requires a longer 'essay style' response. This should be a personal evaluation but make sure opinion is fully justified.

# Exam skills: notes

The notes you are able to take into the exam for Section B will be extremely useful to you. If they are prepared carefully they will provide you with guidance and support when responding to the questions. You can be thinking about your notes from the moment you have your live production experience. It is important to jot down your thoughts and ideas as soon as possible so that they can be carefully prepared for the exam.

## Preparing the notes

You must ensure you prepare your final notes under the appropriate conditions.

- You can have 500 words handwritten or typed.
- They may include sketches, drawings and diagrams if required.
- They can only reference the one performance you have seen that you intend to write about.
- They cannot reference any other part of the exam.
- The final notes must be made with no internet access and under the supervision of your teacher.
- You can use any original notes you made on the performance.
- Your teacher will collect the completed notes.
- Your notes will be given back to you on the day of your exam.
- You will be able to use your original notes to revise for the exam, although obviously you won't have the 500 words that you handed in to your teacher.

## Contents of notes

Avoid any unnecessary words in your notes. Use sketches and diagrams where possible. You must not think that the notes are a replacement for revision. They are a useful added tool for you to be able to present your knowledge and understanding of the live performance. They can include information about the following:

- the performers (their names and roles)
- costume design
- set design
- lighting design
- sound design, including music
- the director's overall concept/interpretation
- performance style
- use of stage space
- impact on you as an individual audience member
- impact on the audience as a whole.

# Exam skills: revision

The written exam has been created to test the knowledge and understanding you acquire over the whole course. During all the practical work:

- try to keep in mind that you will have an exam at the end
- find ways to collect knowledge and store notes so they will be useful when you come to revise.

This knowledge may include:

- practical skills
- drama terminology
- information about the text you explore in preparation for Section A
- details about the live production you see for Section B.

Try to link together what you know so that you can show your understanding of drama as a whole.

## Building and testing your knowledge

Make time throughout the course to recap what you have learned. Some of the techniques below might help you.

- **Summary notes**: whether you prefer cue cards or writing onto a note pad, summarising what you have learned is essential. Making summary notes is an active way of going over a lot of material. Simply re-reading the textbook or your previous notes will not place the knowledge into your long-term memory.
- **Organising your thinking**: the exam will be testing your knowledge and understanding. It is important that your thoughts and ideas are organised appropriately. Making connections between all the things you know will showcase your understanding. Try planning for a past paper question by placing relevant cue cards on the floor in the structure you think will best answer the question.
- **Re-reading your text**: it is invaluable to read your Section A text as many times as you can before the exam. Try re-reading it with a group of friends and discussing key moments that you have learned in lesson time. You could prepare a series of still images of the key moments to test your memory as a group. Read the words out loud, even if you are on your own, and bring the characters to life.
- **Repetition and testing**: keep going over your notes, and keep testing your knowledge and understanding.

Drama is an exciting subject that will give you the chance to build an appreciation of work of all of those involved in taking the words of a play and reproducing them, in a meaningful and creative way, in a live performance. Give yourself plenty of time to revise. Go over things as many times as you need to. Test yourself, and get others to test you too. You will be developing skills in your study of this subject that will last you a lifetime.

## Overview of Section A

You are asked to show your knowledge and understanding of the work of those involved in creating a production of a play for an audience. The phrase 'page to stage' indicates the journey from the very first reading of the play text to the first performance for an audience. Your teacher will choose your Section A text and will lead you in exploring this text practically to enable you to write about bringing the text to life, as a performer, designer and/or director. Your journey through Section A will mirror the process that professional theatre makers undertake. Questions will ask you to consider how you would create meaning for an audience and bring a play to life. This is the largest section of the written exam: it is worth 45 of the 60 marks available. This part of the exam forms 30% of the whole GCSE.

Below are the eight performance texts you can choose from to write about in your Component 3 exam: four written before 1954 and four written after 2000. Your teacher will choose one play from this list.

**List A (written before 1954)**

| Title and playwright | Genre |
| --- | --- |
| *An Inspector Calls* by J.B. Priestley | Social thriller/mystery |
| *The Crucible* by Arthur Miller | Historical drama |
| *Government Inspector* by Nikolai Gogol (adapted by David Harrower) | Black comedy |
| *Twelfth Night* by William Shakespeare | Romantic comedy |

**List B (written after 2000)**

| Title and playwright | Genre |
| --- | --- |
| *1984* (adapted from the novel by George Orwell) by Robert Icke and Duncan Macmillan | Political satire |
| *Blue Stockings* by Jessica Swale | Historical drama |
| *DNA* by Dennis Kelly | Black comedy |
| *Dr Korczak's Example* by David Grieg | Historical drama |

This section of the book will focus on performance texts for Component 3 and how you can prepare for the exam, but some of the exercises may also help to prepare you in other parts of the course – for example, when studying your text for performance in Component 2.

## Studying the text in preparation for the written exam

You will work with your teacher and other students in your group to explore how actors, directors and designers work on a performance text. This will involve:

- directing scenes to explore rehearsal techniques
- developing and performing a character
- working on voice and movement skills
- experimenting with ideas for designing costumes, lighting, set or sound.

Throughout the course you will learn how theatre makers bring a text to life for an audience. You should know the text very well. When you take your exam you should be able to place the extract in the context of the whole text.

## In your exam

An extract of about 80–100 lines from your performance text will be printed on the exam paper. The questions will ask you to write from the viewpoint of the different theatre makers: **performer**, **director and designer**.

You will answer a total of **five** questions about your chosen performance text. You will be marked on your ability to **demonstrate knowledge and understanding of how drama and theatre is developed and performed**. This means your answers should show that you can write confidently and perceptively about how the skills of performers, directors and designers bring a text to life. The exam questions ask you to respond as though you were acting, directing or designing and to write about your ideas, justifying them with accurate reference to the performance text. The questions are worth different amounts of marks so you need to plan your time carefully.

**What are the marks for each question?**

| Question | How many marks? |
| --- | --- |
| (a)(i) | 4 |
| (a)(ii) | 6 |
| (b)(i) | 9 |
| (b)(ii) | 12 |
| (c) | 14 |

**Exam tip**

For question (b)(ii) make sure you refer to the complete performance text in your answer.

**Exam tip**

You will not be able to take your performance text into the exam. Make sure you are so familiar with it that you know exactly which part the printed section comes from. For any extract you are given, make sure you can answer these questions.

- What is happening in this extract?
- What happened earlier in the text?
- At this point, what does the audience know about the plot and characters?

**Exam tip**

Practise planning your time by answering questions with different mark allocations so that you know how long to spend on a 4-mark answer as opposed to a 14-mark answer. In the exam you can answer the questions in any order, as long as you label them correctly – for example, Q1 (b)(ii).

## From page to stage

### First approaches to a performance text

The first time a performance text is read by actors, director and design team their theatrical imagination is sparked. Each individual begins the creative journey of putting the text on stage. The different theatre makers include:

- the director
- the actors (performers)
- the designers of the **production elements**: set, properties, costumes, lighting and sound.

Each specialist will approach the performance text in a slightly different way. The director will have an overview of the whole production. They might:

- have fixed ideas of how the text will be presented, or
- allow decisions to emerge during the first reading.

For example, in 1992 Stephen Daldry directed a landmark production of *An Inspector Calls*. He approached the play knowing he wanted to emphasise how people should take responsibility for each other in modern society.

Another example is Lucy Bailey, who directed *Twelfth Night* at the Manchester Royal Exchange. She chose to set the play in a seedy hotel, where people are 'washed up' and thrown together in unreal circumstances.

Actors will focus initially on:

- their own role, and
- the way the character develops during the play.

For example, two characters in *Blue Stockings* are based on real people. So the actors might begin by researching the lives of these individuals.

Another example is *1984* – a reworking of George Orwell's novel. Here, an actor would read the novel to gain an insight into character.

On a first reading designers would note the 'given' information:

- locations
- period
- times of day
- sounds indicated in the text.

They would also begin to shape some creative ideas about their own production element.

### Top tip

You will be exploring your text in class with your teacher. As you work through the different scenes and characters, you could keep notes on your thoughts about the:

- directing elements
- performing elements
- production elements.

These notes may come in useful later. You could style your notes like the ones in the 'Designer's notes' box below.

Below is an example of a costume designer's first thoughts about costumes for Malvolio in *Twelfth Night*. The director had decided on a contemporary setting for the play. The costume designer uses this detail to think how Malvolio might be dressed.

### Designer's notes

*Themes:* love, deception, migration.

*Character:* Malvolio (described by others as sad and civil, poor fool, virtuous, a turkey-cock, Puritan).

*Modern dress:* three-piece pinstriped suit, maybe glasses, bowler hat? Formal. Two pairs stockings – yellow. Act 4 Scene 2, yellow cross-hatched knee-length stockings, patent leather shoes, tight leather trousers.

### The director

The director has an overview of the whole production, from the interpretation of the playwright's text for a modern audience to final decisions about lighting and costume.

The director is more than the person who tells actors where to stand! The role encompasses all the production elements, which involves:

- working with designers, and
- shaping the performance text with the actors.

(These aspects are discussed in detail later in this section.)

One of the first things a director will look for is a **director's concept** for their production. The decision will be based on:

- how the text can be made relevant to the audience
- what kind of impact the director wants to have on an audience
- the opportunities presented by the stage space in the theatre.

For example, Richard Jones's 2011 production of *Government Inspector* at The Young Vic in London, interpreted the play as a wild fantasy. His costumes, set and sound effects gave the play a bizarre quality similar to anarchic television comedies. The style engaged the audience while highlighting how people are willing to be deceived and let corruption flourish.

See also the 'Director's notes' for the concept of *An Inspector Calls* below.

> ### Glossary
>
> **Director's concept**: How the director imagines the text and its themes, ideas, mood and design, in order to have an impact on the audience.

### Director's notes

*Concept for An Inspector Calls*

*Politics: Thatcher 'no such thing as society'.*

*Message of the play: 'We don't live alone — we are dependent on one another.'*

*Expressionist design: audience is looking into the lives of the Birlings — the house like a doll's house on stilts with the front removed. The house collapses as the Birling family falls apart.*

*Wasteland surrounding the house is a place where anything can happen. Witnesses from 1940s in the wasteland watching the action representing the working class who are not in the play.*

*Past, present, future co-exist.*

*Stereotypical middle-class characters — largely unlikeable. Inspector Goole is other-worldly and dressed in 1940s costume as if he has come from the future.*

### Activity ?

Do this activity after you have read your chosen performance text.

Create a 'mind map' of how you see the text.

Include: the impact you want to have on your audience; important meanings you want to emphasise; the acting style; and how the production elements will be used.

# Section A Bringing texts to life

For your written exam, you will need to write from the viewpoint of a director about your intended impact and meaning. The question may ask about the way you will:

- enhance the production for an audience, or
- bring the extract to life for an audience.

Here is an example of director's notes about how they think they might stage a specific scene. Thinking in this way will help you to be able to answer the questions in the exam.

## Director's notes

As a director of **The Crucible** I would employ the production elements of sound and music to highlight the emotional climax in this scene to engage the audience in the agony of John Proctor as he fights with his conscience. As the sun rises, casting a shaft of warm light into the cell, the distant sound of birds represents freedom while a continuous, discordant note mirrors Proctor's inner tension.

## Directing: working with actors

A director works with actors to explore the intentions of the character. A director encourages actors to:

- look carefully at the text
- develop different approaches to the text
- make decisions about what their character wants from each moment
- develop relationships between other characters during rehearsals.

Directors use a range of **rehearsal techniques** to bring a play to life on stage. You might recognise some of these techniques from your drama lessons. These techniques might include:

- improvising a scene that is discussed but not scripted
- examining the text to gain insight into characters by looking at what they say about themselves and what others say about them
- asking actors to say exactly what they **want** on each line – for example: 'I want to **belittle** you' or 'I want to **tease** you' (this informs intonation and sometimes movement)
- 'immediate circumstances' – what might have happened **before** the scene or entrance such as the character's journey, the weather or a conversation
- 'emotion memory' – where the actor remembers a similar event in their own life and uses this memory to feel the emotion of their character.

## Glossary

**Rehearsal techniques**: Strategies, exercises and activities used by a director to explore possible approaches to the scene, the character or the relationships during rehearsals.

## Top tip

You won't actually be asked about rehearsal techniques in your exam, but the techniques opposite will help you to explore your text in the same way that actors do. You might also use some of these techniques in class.

Bringing texts to life

## Taking it further

**Example**: In a rehearsal for *Blue Stockings* the director worked on Act 2, Scenes 4 and 7 with the actors playing Mrs Welsh and Miss Blake. In Scene 4, Mrs Welsh forbids Miss Blake from encouraging the girls to attend a suffragist rally. Then in Scene 7 Miss Blake tells Mr Banks she has resigned. There is no argument scripted in the play, but the actors imagined and improvised a scene where Miss Blake argues with Mrs Welsh and resigns.

The improvisation started with the final line of Scene 4, when Miss Blake says: 'Please. Please don't ask me to choose.' The actors improvised what they imagined had been said and why Miss Blake resigned. This helped the actor playing Miss Blake to recall her emotion when she retells the event in Scene 7.

**Explore**: In class, with your teacher, try an improvisation like the example above to get to know your text better. Are there any conversations or events that have not been scripted in your text but that may help you to get to know the characters better? Remember, you won't have to answer questions about rehearsal techniques in your exam. The focus of your exam will be the performance.

One technique the director Max Stafford-Clarke uses is to hand out playing cards to the actors. All picture cards are removed, leaving 1–10 in the two red and two black suits. Red cards indicate a character in favour of something, while black cards indicate opposition. The number on the card indicates the strength of response.

Actors are given a card face down so no one else can see it. The card gives them clues about their attitude towards something, for example, a red 10 would mean you were strongly in favour, while a black 3 would mean you were only somewhat against the given issue. For example, in a rehearsal for the play *1984*, actors were told their card represented how they felt about freedom of the press. Each actor then took turns to argue their viewpoint in the rehearsal room.

## Activity

With a partner, direct an extract from your chosen performance text.

1   Choose a scene of no more than 100 lines.
2   Discuss what this extract means to you and how you would want the audience to be affected by it.
3   Now decide on two rehearsal strategies you might use with actors for this extract.

## Directing: working with the set designer

The director will meet the designers to:

- share their vision for the play
- explore the restrictions and possibilities of the theatre space.

Different specialists design costumes, sound, compose original music and design the lighting. The director must ensure that overall design has an impact

## Taking it further

- Look at the website for Max Stafford-Clarke's theatre company, Out of Joint. Find out more about his rehearsal techniques.

- If you have an opportunity, stay for a post-show discussion when you next go to the theatre.

- Research Jeremy Herrin at Headlong Theatre. Learn more about the company's inventive ideas and creative rehearsal strategies.

## Exam tip

Whenever you make notes on your play try to keep them somewhere all together. They will be really useful when you come to revise.

## Glossary

**Proscenium arch**: The proscenium is a semi-permanent wall that divides the stage from the audience. The opening in the wall frames the stage. This opening is known as the proscenium arch.

**In-the-round**: The audience is placed on all four sides of the acting space or in a circle.

**Thrust stage**: The audience is seated on three sides as though the stage has 'thrust' out into the auditorium.

on the audience. Often people recall what they see more than what they hear. So a set must reflect the meaning, mood and atmosphere of the text.

Initial discussions focus on the director's ideas for using the theatre space and the audience's position in relation to the action. Designers use these ideas to be inventive with theatre spaces. For example, at the Old Vic (which is a traditional, ornate **proscenium** arch theatre), the designer of *The Crucible* placed the audience on the stage, creating an intimate **in-the-round** theatre.

Sometimes the shape of the auditorium is an important feature of the production. For example:

- the Globe (where *Blue Stockings* was first performed) is a reconstructed Elizabethan theatre with a **thrust stage**
- Manchester Royal Exchange has a modern theatre-in-the-round space.

The positioning of the entrances and exits in these spaces provides many exciting possibilities.

The designer and director also examine:

- the mood and atmosphere of the production
- the important locations in the play.

For example, for his RSC production of *Twelfth Night* in 2012, director David Farr made links with the London Olympics. What he found interesting about the Olympics was that people arrived in one location from many different places for a short but intense time together. His setting was a hotel and the costumes were modern.

Ian MacNeil's set design for *An Inspector Calls* at the National Theatre.

Another example is Ian MacNeil's set design for *An Inspector Calls*, which has become world famous – mainly because it set the play in a **box set** drawing room. The director, Stephen Daldry, wanted the set to show that time and landscapes could be manipulated. The house opened up, allowing the audience to see into the cocooned upper-class world, while people with less wealth were literally and metaphorically 'out in the cold' on the harsh cobbled streets. The play finished as the house famously crumbled before the audience's eyes, symbolising the downfall of the Birling family.

### Glossary

**Box set**: The creation of an interior room with three walls.

This example shows how closely the designer and director work to achieve a cohesive production.

## Performing: characterisation

'Characterisation' describes the process an actor undertakes to interpret a role. This is why no two performances of the same role will be the same. Actors:

- research the role
- think about how the character they are playing develops during the play
- consider their relationship with other characters
- consider how their character contributes to the story and meaning of the play.

Their decisions will be shown through their performance skills (for example, voice, physicality, movement, gesture and facial expression) to communicate their interpretation of a role to an audience.

## Working on characterisation

An actor needs to 'get to know' their character and 'get inside their mind' before they can truthfully perform the role. Here are some questions an actor might consider about their character when they are getting to know them:

- What has happened to me before the play begins?
- What do I look like?
- What is my motivation?
- What do I want at key times in the play?
- How do I feel about other characters?
- How do I see myself?
- How do other people see me?
- How do I change during the play?
- Who do I like and dislike?

Rehearsal is the practical exploration of the play text where performers develop characters. The rehearsal process informs the way performers use voice, movement and stage space. These activities will help you to dig deeper into your performance text.

### Activity ?

Choose a character from your performance text.

1   Consider a few words to describe the character and write them down.
2   Choose just three of those words and list them underneath your notes in capital letters.
3   In Dennis Kelly's *DNA*, three words that could be used to describe John Tate are: MENACING, DETACHED, CALLOUS (see photograph). Look again at your three words. Are you happy with them? Do they give a good enough character description?

### Exam tip

Although these exercises will help you to get to know your text, your exam will only be about the performance itself. It will not ask you about preparation for a performance or ask you to explain how other people prepare.

# Section A Bringing texts to life

**Activity** ?

Using the character you chose in the previous activity and your knowledge of the text, what questions do you have about the character? Make a list, and jot down any answers you can think of.

**Activity** ?

From your performance text, choose an extract of about 100 lines with two to four characters.

1  Working in a group, divide the extract into short sections and give each section a title.

2  Choose a character each.

3  Working on your own, write down what your character wants in each section. Keep this information secret.

4  As a group, rehearse the scene and think only about how performance skills (voice, movement, gesture, eye contact) convey what you want.

5  Discuss what you think the other characters wanted. How did you know? How did their performances make your character feel?

6  Make notes to describe these performance skills as though you were answering an exam question.

This activity will help you to understand how an actor prepares for a role. Remember, though, that the focus of your exam will be on the performance itself and not the preparation. You will not have to answer any questions on rehearsal techniques.

An actor would begin by examining the text for valuable information about the character. One method that reveals this information is to look at what the character says about other characters and what others say about him or her.

Here is an example of an actor playing John Proctor in *The Crucible*.

| Character | What I say about myself | What others say about me |
|---|---|---|
| Proctor | 'I cannot mount the gibbet like a saint … I am not that man' | '… this man has struck me true' |

There are many exercises actors can use to get to know their character. For instance, a scene can be divided into small sections, each covering one topic or idea. These sections are given titles. When the whole scene is played the actors use movement, voice and gesture to convey what they want according to the titles. The different 'wants' from all the characters can be used to create dramatic tension.

For example, in *Blue Stockings* the character Maeve is a student at Cambridge University who comes from a poor family. In one section her brother, Billy, arrives to bring the news that her mother has died, which means she must go home to look after the family. The section is titled *Mother is dead*. Each actor decides what their character **wants**. The actor playing Billy decides, *I want Maeve to come home*.

If actors are playing real people, as in *Dr Korczak's Example* or *The Crucible*, they would research the life of that individual and bring that information to the performance.

## Performing: voice and movement

An actor's voice is the main instrument for telling the story to the audience. It:

• communicates a range of emotions

• reveals character traits.

The voice has often been described as an 'instrument' because it can be used in various ways to create a musicality that belongs to the character. In your exam you will be asked to consider how a performer uses voice to convey character or emotion. The terms in the 'vocabulary of voice' box explain how an actor's voice might be described. For example, in *Blue Stockings* the performer playing Billy speaks slowly in a low-pitched, menacing tone when he insists Maeve leaves the university. He uses a regional accent to indicate his class.

## Vocabulary of voice

**Tone**: The 'colour' or emotional quality of the voice (for example, menacing, sharp, jolly, rousing, strident, soothing).

**Monotone**: Speaking without variations in tone (for example, toneless, dull, expressionless).

**Intonation**: The rise and fall in the speaking of a line or speech.

**Pitch**: The highness or lowness of a vocal tone – (for example, shrill, piercing, deep).

**Inflection**: Varying the pitch during a line or speech.

**Volume**: How loudly or quietly the actor speaks (for example, whisper, shout, soft, screech, yell).

**Accent**: Indicates the region the character comes from (for example, Cockney, French, Liverpudlian, Cornish).

**Pace**: How quickly or slowly the lines are spoken (for example, staccato, steady, measured, slow).

### Glossary

**Actioning**: A rehearsal technique developed by a renowned director that examines the intentions of the characters.

## Using your voice to build a character

There are several things to consider when choosing a voice for a role, for example:

- age
- status
- confidence
- vocal mannerisms (such as a nervous giggle)
- the play's genre.

An actor's voice is determined by the impact they want to have on:

- other characters
- the audience.

Director Max Stafford-Clarke uses an exercise called 'actioning', to help explore a text during rehearsal. For each line, or part of a line, the actor decides what effect they want to have – such as, 'I want to patronise you.' So the action would be 'patronises' and the actor would write this before the line.

This is how the above example looks in the text for *An Inspector Calls* when Birling first meets the inspector.

**Birling [*patronises*]**: You're new aren't you?

The action will determine the way the actor uses their voice. So Birling, for example, may speak sneeringly in a low tone at a measured tempo.

### Activity

Read the actioned extract from *Twelfth Night* (Act 3, Scene 4) below.

**Olivia**: *charms* Here, wear this jewel for me, *encourages* 'tis my picture; *entreats* Refuse it not; *amuses* it hath no tongue to vex you;
*urges* And I beseech you come again to-morrow.
*tempts* What shall you ask of me that I'll deny,
That honour saved may upon asking give?
**Viola**: *Stops* Nothing but this;
*instructs* your true love for my master.

1   Choose a very short extract from your performance text and 'action' it with a partner or group.
2   Now play the extract using the appropriate voice to convey the actions.

# Section A Bringing texts to life

Now try this exam-style question, and look at one student's answer below. As you read, keep in mind how you might also respond. (The answer here is not intended to be perfect. It's to help you understand how you could improve your own work.) Look also at the photograph of a scene being played between Olivia and Viola.

## Exam-style question

You are going to play Olivia (from *Twelfth Night*). Explain two ways you would use vocal skills to play this character in the extract below:

**Olivia**: Here, wear this jewel for me, 'tis my picture;
Refuse it not; it hath no tongue to vex you;
And I beseech you come again to-morrow.
What shall you ask of me that I'll deny,
That honour saved may upon asking give?
**Viola**: *Stops* Nothing but this; *instructs* your true love for my master. **(4 marks)**

## Top tip

As you read the student answers in these pages, keep in mind how you might also respond to the questions. The answers here are not intended to be perfect. They are to help you understand how you could improve your own work.

An actor's **physicality** contributes to:

- the audience's understanding of the character's status, emotions and relationships
- the mood and setting of the scene.

For example, an actor playing Betty Parris in Act 3 of *The Crucible* would use physical skills to show:

- her terror
- the power Abigail has
- that she is copying Mary Warren's gestures.

Judi Dench (right) and Lisa Harrow in a 1969 production of Shakespeare's *Twelfth Night*.

## Student answer

*The first way I would use vocal skills would be to work on the tone of my voice as Olivia. For example, I would use a soft deep tone on the line 'wear this jewel for me', showing that Olivia wants to persuade Viola to visit again. I would then speak more quickly and sharply to say the line 'come again to-morrow' to Viola. This would show that Olivia really wants Viola to come back. When Olivia tries to charm Viola with 'What shall you ask …', I would talk in a measured way with a flirty tone. That would be OK, because Olivia has a higher status than Viola. So she would be able to flirt. She would be able to control the situation better than Viola.*

In your exam you will be asked to consider how a performer uses physical skills to convey character or emotion. The terms in the 'vocabulary of physicality' box can be used to explain how an actor uses movement, gesture and stillness in a performance.

Here is an example of an exam-style question about physical skills, followed by one student's answer. As you read, keep in mind how you might also respond. (The answer here is not intended to be perfect. It's to help you understand how you could improve your own work.)

## Glossary

**Physicality**: An actor's use of their body, including moving across the stage, posture, gestures, the face and eyes.

## Exam-style question

You are playing the role of Betty Parris in this extract. How would you use physical skills to show her emotions in this scene?

## Student answer

*If I was playing Betty Parris in this scene I would show that I understand Abigail's plan by I making brief eye contact with the other girls to show that we all knew what we had to do. My gestures would mirror Mary Warren's: for example if she pointed at Abigail I would point in exactly the same way. I would also speak exactly as Mary Warren speaks, copying her volume, intonation and pace. My facial expression would show that I was afraid and I would show this by widening my eyes and frowning whilst copying Mary Warren's vocal tone and movements exactly.*

## Vocabulary of physicality

**Posture**: The way actors hold their body when standing, sitting or moving.

**Gesture**: A movement (especially of the hand or head) to express an idea or meaning, a feeling or intention.

**Facial expression**: Use of the face to convey emotion or reaction.

**Eye contact**: A moment when eyes meet. The length of the eye contact can convey emotion and status.

**Speed/pace**: How quickly the actor moves in the space.

**Stillness**: When an actor is silent, calm and not moving.

**Mannerisms**: Repeated movements and gestures that are a feature of the character.

**Non-verbal communication:** How actors can show meaning without actually speaking words. All of the above are forms of non-verbal communication.

## Exam-style question

Extract: from Act 2

from Mrs Birling: 'I'm talking to the Inspector', to Sheila: 'Stop it, please, Mother'.

You are going to play Mrs Birling (in the above extract from *An Inspector Calls*). As a performer, explain two ways you would use physical skills to play this character. You must provide a reason for each suggestion.    **(6 marks)**

## Student answer

*If I were playing Mrs Birling in this section I would use physical skills to emphasise my status. I would turn suddenly and move quickly towards Sheila on 'I'm talking to the Inspector'. I would do this to put Sheila in her place, showing that I am in charge. I would pause, turn and stand very stiffly and proudly making eye contact with the Inspector and walk at a slow, measured pace right up to him. I would do this to try to intimidate him as I am used to others being impressed by the Birlings. When I ask if he know that my husband was Lord Mayor I would sweep away to a commanding position in the centre of the room, addressing the Inspector without facing him. I would turn threateningly and face him on 'and he's still a magistrate'. This is to show that I feel he should be afraid of my husband's power.*

## Exam tips

When writing about your ideas for physicality, try to picture what is happening on the stage and describe what the actor's body is doing.

Your writing needs to be in the first person. For example, 'If I were directing the actor playing Betty …', or 'As Gerald, my facial expression would be …'.

You should also think back to any practical work you have done as a class on your set text. For example, you might already have thought about how some of the characters would use physicality, and why.

# Design: set design and staging

The set designer transforms the performance space into another world, which characters will inhabit to tell the story to an audience. The set:

- gives a visual key to the audience about the themes highlighted in the production
- reflects concept and style, as well as the time of day, location, season and historical period
- establishes the mood and atmosphere of the production
- offers creative possibilities for the movement and grouping of the actors.

# Section A Bringing texts to life

The designer builds a scale model of the set, called a model box. This is taken to rehearsals to give the actors an idea of what the set will look like. A mood board is used by designers to capture their initial ideas. It includes images, fabrics and materials that capture the essence of the play.

## Vocabulary of set design

**Shape**: The geometric appearance (for example, angular, curved, pointed, rugged, silhouetted).

**Materials**: The medium or fabric (for example, metal, glass, wood, velvet, sacking, brocade).

**Colour**: The shades and tones (for example, crimson, russet, golden, azure, flaxen, bright, subtle, hint).

**Texture**: The feel and appearance of the surface (for example, rough, coarse, rippled, smooth, grainy).

**Cyclorama**: A cloth stretched tight around the back of a stage set, often used to depict the sky.

**Back projection**: Digital scenic effects projected onto a screen to signify location or mood.

**Abstract**: Not representing reality (for example, uses shapes, colour and textures to suggest mood/location).

**Naturalistic**: Recreates the location in exact detail, making it appear real.

Below is an example of an exam-style question about design.

### Exam-style question

Discuss how you would use one design element to enhance the production of this extract [given in the actual exam paper] for the audience. **(14 marks)**

This student has chosen set design for *1984*. Look at their planning notes below.

### Student notes

*Locations:* Panelled room, Corridor, Canteen, Countryside, Antique shop, O'Brien's Apartment, Room 101, Café

*Atmosphere/mood:* Sinister, Threatening, Disorientating

*Shape/colour/texture:* Sharp, Bright, Edgy, Wood (panelled room), Clinical (Room 101), Musty (antique shop)

### Activity ?

On a large sheet of plain, white paper create some visual ideas for your performance text. Use the example above to help.

1   Look through magazines, or online, for images that reflect your ideas. Cut them out or print them and attach to your plan.
2   Try adding materials and textures – for example, sand, leaves, plastic, velvet or denim.

A designer's mood board.

# Design: costume

A costume designer will liaise with both the set designer and the lighting designer to realise the director's ideas for the production. Costume tells the audience about when and where the play is set. For example, dresses with an empire waist made of light fabrics in light colours place a play in the early 18th century.

Directors frequently set plays in a different period, so costume locates the chosen era for the audience. A character's costume:

- communicates age, status and personality
- communicates economic climate
- can be symbolic (indicating an aspect of the production rather than reflecting character)
- needs to be practical so that it does not restrict the character's action.

Even when characters appear to be wearing 'everyday clothes', designers will have paid attention to the exact details.

Olivia #1
'veiled'
Dark full, wavy hair.
Black/Midnight Blue – Fellini
Black striped straw hat – HUGE
Jackie O sunglasses
Black chiffon (sheer) blouse
Full Bishop sleeve w/slits over front of arm
Black brocade 'corset' – jet buttons, etc.
Black silk satin sash
Black burnout velvet – skirt
w/black lace ruffles
Skirt splits in front to reveal …
Black satin capri length cigarette pants
black patent leather pumps
* blouse and skirt are sheer

KC 12th Night USF '13

## Activity ?

Look at the costume sketch for Olivia in *Twelfth Night*. Notice the difference in the two halves, then answer these questions.

1 What does this design sketch tell you about Olivia?

2 Imagine you are in the audience when this character enters. What do you think the character is like?

3 Comment on style, colour, hair and accessories. What is the location, the period, weather?

The use of textures and materials signify key messages to the audience, for example:

- a character dressed in velvet would immediately show wealth, whereas
- a character in shabby, torn clothes suggests poverty.

Fabric is chosen according to texture, for example:

- satins are smooth and shiny
- lace is light and highly textured.

For extra texture, plastics, leathers, furs, feathers and other materials can be combined with other fabrics. Costumes that need to appear dirty or shabby are 'broken down' after they are made.

# Section A Bringing texts to life

## Vocabulary of costume

**Style**: The concept of the play and overall appearance.

**Period**: The time the play is being set (for example, the 1960s, Elizabethan, post-war Russia).

**Naturalistic**: Accurate to the period.

**Representational**: A single item that indicates a new character (for example, change of hat).

**Symbolic**: Item or colour signals to the audience (for example, white for innocence).

**Character**: For example, personality, status, wealth and confidence.

**Colour to show character trait**: For example, some designs are in tones of a single colour.

**Texture**: The feel of the fabric.

**Fabric**: The materials (for example, silk, brocade, denim, fur, cotton, voile, leather).

**Break down**: Make a costume appear shabby or dirty (for example, after a battle or fight, or a walk in the rain).

**Costume props**: For example, hats, shawls, umbrellas, canes.

## Activity

In your exam you will be asked to suggest how, as a director, you would use costume to bring the extract to life for an audience.

1 Choose a short extract involving two or more characters from your performance text.

2 For two characters, sketch and annotate your initial ideas for costume.

3 Below your sketch write notes showing how these ideas link to your director's concept.

## Design: sound

The use of sound can:

- suggest location, time and weather
- enhance mood and atmosphere
- evoke off-stage events
- be recorded or produced live
- intensify mood and pinpoint an historical era
- provoke an audience response.

Some sound effects, such as doorbells, telephones and battlefields, can drive the narrative. Others, such as ambient sounds, are used to create atmosphere – for example, a slow drum roll underpinning a tragic ending. Digital technology offers a range of opportunities for inventive sound design.

The sound designer examines the text for sounds clues. Examples include:

- an actor speaking the line 'Listen to the birdsong'
- a note from the playwright that says: *A gun shot is heard off stage.*

The director's decisions may have implication for sound. For example, if *Twelfth Night* is set in the 1920s, music will be important to suggest the era. In Headlong's production of *1984*, abstract sound was used to disorientate the audience.

Here is an exam-style question about design. Look also at the student answer, who has chosen sound as their design element. As you read, keep in mind how you might also respond. (The answer here is not intended to be perfect. It's to help you understand how you could improve your own work.)

## Exam-style question

Discuss how you would use one design element to enhance the production of this extract from *The Crucible* for the audience.

**Elizabeth** (*with great fear*): I will fear nothing. (*She looks about the room as though to fix it in her mind.*) Tell the children I have gone to visit someone sick.

*She walks out the door. For a moment Proctor watches her from the doorway. The clank of chains is heard*

**Proctor**: Herrick! Herrick, don't chain her! (*He rushes out the door. From outside:* Damn you, man you will not chain her! Off with them! I'll not have it I will not have her chained!*)

............

*There are other men's voices against his. Hale, in a fever of guilt and uncertainty, turns from the door to avoid the sight: Mary Warren bursts into tears and sits weeping: Giles Corey calls to Hale.*

**Herrick** (*panting*): In God's name. John, I cannot help myself. I must chain them all. Now let you keep inside this house till I am gone! (*He goes out with his deputies.*)

*Proctor stands there, gulping air. Horses and wagon creaking are heard.*   **(14 marks)**

## Student answer

*The sound in this extract has several functions. It helps the audience to picture the action off stage, builds the tension and evokes an emotional response in the audience. I would use exaggerated and echoing sound effects of live clanking chains following Elizabeth's exit. This would play on the audience's emotions as they picture the innocent Elizabeth roughly chained up. This effect would be created off stage with heavy chains and would overlap with a recorded burst of noisy and disorderly men's voice's. The chains would be very loud and make the audience feel uneasy as they picture Elizabeth is being roughly handled. I would use live sound for the chains so that it feels very close to the audience but the men's voices would be recorded because I would want to suggest that there were several men outside and with recorded sound I could create different layers and tones. The sound of voices and an occasional clank of chains reduce in volume to show that the cart is moving away towards the prison.*

**Exam tip**

In your exam you will be expected to support the decisions you made with reasons. For example, why did you choose live or recorded sound or music? What was your intention for the use of a particular sound effect or piece of music at specific times in the extract?

## Design: lighting

The lighting designer will work with costume and set designers to create the mood and atmosphere of the production. The most important function of stage lighting is to ensure that the audience can see. Never write about 'dark lighting'!

Lighting can:

- convey the weather
- convey the time of day
- add to a key moment
- draw attention to an actor.

Large professional theatres have very complex lighting systems but small touring companies and fringe venues can create extremely effective designs with a simple lighting kit.

Lighting designers must consider the:

- source of the light – a window, a torch, a fire, candle or table lamp, an overhead light
- the quality of light – warm summer sunlight; a cold, frosty winter night.

Light can also be used in an abstract way to have an impact on the audience. Colour is the key to creating the mood or directing the emotion of the audience.

Read through the exam-style question and answer below. Remember that the answer here is not intended to be perfect – it's to help you understand how you could improve your own work.

### Vocabulary of lighting design

**Spotlight**: A lantern that can focus a beam of light onto a specific place or actor.

**Backlit**: Light coming from behind the action. This can create silhouettes.

**Crossfade**: One lighting state fades down and another fades up, without darkness.

**Blackout**: A sudden or slow fading out of the lighting.

**Gel**: Filters on lanterns that create different colours of lighting.

**Gobo**: A plate shape placed in front of a spotlight to create a shape on the stage.

**Intensity**: The brightness or softness of the light.

**Direction**: Where the light is coming from – the source of lighting.

# Section A Bringing texts to life

## Activity

Select an extract of about 100 lines from your performance text where you think lighting will be important. Work in a small group.

1   Search online for images of lighting for plays with similar themes, settings or historical periods.

2   Note the essential features (for example, time, location), then discuss ideas for colour, mood, atmosphere and special effects.

3   Create a mood board on sugar paper or a Pinterest board on your computer.

4   Working on your own, write an answer to the exam-style question opposite using the information you have gathered about lighting.

## Exam-style question

Discuss how you would use one design element to enhance the production of this extract [given in the exam paper] for the audience.
**(14 marks)**

## Activity

Choose a section of your performance text that you have worked on with your teacher.

1   Make a chart with four columns.

2   Write these titles on each column:
    line/moment   effect   reason   audience

3   In the first column write the line or moment to indicate where the lighting effect occurs.

4   In the second column write what the effect is and how it will be created (for example, type of lantern, gobo, gel, speed of effect).

5   In the third column write the reason why you have chosen this effect.

6   In the fourth column write about the impact this lighting effect has on the audience.

| Line/ moment | Effect | Reason | Audience |
|---|---|---|---|
|  |  |  |  |
|  |  |  |  |
|  |  |  |  |
|  |  |  |  |
|  |  |  |  |

## Student answer

The lighting for this extract must indicate that it is late evening, establish that interior lighting was from lamps and candles and that heat and cooking used open fires. I would enhance the production of the extract by creating a warm and homely glow in the room. This would contrast sharply with the hostile cold outside when the door is opened and Elizabeth is taken away. The warm light would come from the fire and from a candle on the table and a lamp, brought in by John Proctor, hung on a wall. The candle would be a Rosco flicker candle with realistic flame and dripping wax and operated by a 9v battery: this would meet health and safety requirements. It would be lit by a hard edged Profile spotlight with a Medium Amber filter. There would be an area of warmth at the table. The lantern on the wall would have a classic look but be operated by a 9v battery that makes it safe to hang on the set. The area around the lantern would be lit with a Fresnel spot with a soft edge and an Amber filter. I would make the fire flicker and cast warm shadows around the room. I would create this effect with a Flicker Flame, a rotating metal disc with slots cut out through which light is shone onto a prism-type piece of glass which scatters the beam of light. The gel I would use here is Deep Amber as it gives a firelight glow. The room would have areas of shadow as there are only 3 sources of light.

When the door opens and Elizabeth is led out I would want the lighting to contrast with the warm home. I would light outside the door with a backlighting of Fresnels with Light Steel Blue gels to create moonlight. One area would be more intense than the others to suggest the direction of the moon's beam.

## Properties and stage furniture

Properties, usually known as 'props', are the objects held and used by actors during the performance. Props help to convey the:

- mood of the play
- taste of the characters (and as such can help to make significant statements).

Properties can be divided into several categories.

- Small props are referred to as hand props. These are often used by more than one actor and many of them are indicated in the text. For example, in *Government Inspector* the money given in bribes is a hand prop. A book, a gun, a pen and a wine glass are other examples of hand props.
- Costume props include fans, jewellery, armour and briefcases. These require special consideration from both the director and costume designer because the style needs to match overall design and character decisions.
- Personal props are associated with one actor and may be a feature of the character – for example, a pipe, a cane, or a mirror. Personal props can also indicate rank or status. For example, in *Blue Stockings* Minnie passes through a scene carrying a coal scuttle. Even though she does not light a fire, the prop indicates her status as a servant.

- Some props are also part of the set design. For example, in *The Crucible* the cooking pot over the fire is set. However, when John Proctor stirs and tastes the stew, and Elizabeth serves the meal, it becomes a prop. The set will frequently contain props, such as ornaments, ashtrays or books on shelves, that are used during the performance.
- Stage furniture includes all the furniture on stage and other objects that form part of the set – for example, tables and chairs, desks and any part of the set that actors use to sit or stand on.

An actor will work with the director to decide:

- how to move in the space
- when to sit or stand
- how to engage with the stage furniture.

Some stage furniture can be moved, while other pieces are fixed. Some plays require very little stage furniture. For example, *DNA* is usually performed on an empty stage with a back projection indicating the settings. The actors create levels of visual interest through their positions on the stage. In contrast, *An Inspector Calls* is set in a realistic dining room complete with crockery, glasses, chandeliers, chairs and tables where a dinner party has recently finished.

A backstage props table.

### Activity ?

Note all the stage furniture and properties indicated by the playwright in your chosen performance text. Then choose an extract of about 80 to 100 lines. Imagine you are directing this extract.

1. What stage furniture would you use in your design?
2. How might an actor use the stage during this scene? Give reasons for your choices.
3. Which props (if any) are indicated in the extract?
4. Are there any personal or set props that you would add?
5. How would the props be used in this scene?

## An Inspector Calls by J.B. Priestley

### Performance context

*An Inspector Calls*, written by J.B. Priestley, is set in 1912, just before the outbreak of the First World War (1914–1918), but was first performed in 1945, the year in which the Second World War ended. Priestley fought on the front line in France in the First World War, surviving against the odds only to be faced with another horrific war, the Second World War 1939–1945. The play, although set in the past, looks to the future and argues strongly for a more positive society. Priestley became very concerned about the consequences of social inequality in Britain, and supported the Labour Party in the 1945 election. At the time, *An Inspector Calls* was seen as a political play. The message of the play is simple: we don't live alone, we are members of society and we should be responsible for each other.

The first performance of *An Inspector Calls* was in Moscow in May 1945 by the Kamerny [Chamber] Theatre Company. The first performance in England was on 1st October 1946 at The Old Vic theatre in London. It starred Alec Guiness and Ralph Richardson. The set was a realistic box set on a proscenium arch stage. The set created a dining room complete in every detail. There was a large table with fine china and the remains of dinner. A chandelier over the table, heavy curtains and ornate furnishings showed the Birling's wealth. The lighting was originally designed to show the other-worldly nature of the play with reds and greens but at a late stage in rehearsals this was changed to more naturalistic lighting because the director thought that the audience would be confused. The play was not well received by the critics.

### Edwardian England

The play is set in 1912, just after the Edwardian era (the reign of King Edward VII 1901–1910) ended and George V was crowned. Edward was associated with an era of luxury and opulence. He was part of a fashionable elite and this period is often referred to as the 'Golden Age'. For the working class, though, life was tough. Children died of starvation and the average life span for a working-class man was only 35 years. The poor were not given any financial support, and had to depend on charity. Women were seen as less important than men and did not have the vote. Upper-class women had little choice but to get married, while lower-class women were seen as cheap labour. This inequality between classes and genders sparked an interest in politics: the Suffragettes fought for the vote and unhappy workers threatened factories with strikes. The Edwardian era was, nevertheless, a period during which the British class system was still very rigid. There was little chance for movement from the lower to the upper class.

### The story of *An Inspector Calls*

#### Act 1

The Birling family, headed by Arthur Birling, ex-Lord Mayor and wealthy mill owner, is celebrating his daughter Sheila's engagement to Gerald Croft, the son of a successful business owner.

Inspector Goole arrives and explains that he has come to investigate the death of Eva Smith who died two hours ago in the Infirmary after committing suicide by drinking disinfectant. The Inspector outlines that a

## Taking it further

Carry out some research to find out more about society during the Edwardian era and compare to your findings with events and characters in the play. For example, the Inspector tells Sheila in Act 1 'nineteen-ten – there was a good deal of influenza about.'

chain of events might be responsible for the girl's death, and one by one, each family member learns of the part they played in the girl's death. He shows a photograph of the girl to them individually: they each recognise her but no one else sees the photograph at the same time.

It is first revealed that Eva Smith worked in Arthur Birling's mill. Mr Birling sacked Eva because she was a ringleader in an unsuccessful strike for better pay. Then we learn that Sheila worked in a dress shop and, in a fit of jealousy, had Eva sacked.

## Act 2

The Inspector reveals that Eva changed her name to Daisy Renton. We learn that she had a love affair with Gerald Croft, but he hadn't seen her since they ended their relationship. Sheila reacts to this news about her fiancé by giving Gerald back his engagement ring and he leaves to go for a walk.

The Inspector next questions Mr Birling's wife, Sybil. We find out that Eva Smith came to her while pregnant, to ask for help from a charity committee of which Mrs Birling was chairperson. Mrs Birling used her power to get the committee to refuse to help the girl. She tells the Inspector that the father of the child is the one with whom the true responsibility rests.

## Act 3

Next, Eric, the Birlings' son, is asked about his relationship with Eva Smith. He reveals that he met her in a bar when he was drunk, and then kept her as his mistress. Eva had become pregnant and Eric gave her money that he had stolen from his father's office to help her. Eva broke off the relationship when she discovered the money was stolen.

Now that the truth has been uncovered, the Inspector makes a final speech. He tells the Birlings, 'We don't live alone. We are members of one body. We are responsible for each other.' He exits, leaving the family shocked at the revelations.

At first the Birlings fight among themselves. Sheila wonders whether he was a real police inspector. Gerald returns, having spoken to a policeman on the corner of the street, to tell them, 'That man wasn't a police officer'. The Birlings think that they have been hoaxed. They realise that they could each have been shown a different photograph.

# Section A Bringing texts to life

## Activity ?

### The life of Eva Smith

To help to picture the story, create images of the involvement of each character with Eva Smith in a series of tableau/still images. Caption each image with a quote from the text.

## Taking it further ◥

Research Mary Papadima's 2013 production of the play at the Theatre by the Lake in Keswick, where the ghostly vision of Eva Smith was present on stage.

They call the Infirmary and learn that no girl has died that night, and in fact, the Infirmary has not seen a suicide case for months. Sheila and Eric recognise that they are all guilty in some way, even if all the girls in the Inspector's story were different individuals.

The phone rings. Mr Birling answers it and after a shocked silence says, 'That was the police. A girl has just died – on her way to the Infirmary – after swallowing some disinfectant. And a police officer is on his way here – to ask some questions.'

## Activity ?

### Exploring guilt

In a group of six, read the scene in the play where the Inspector first quizzes each person. Each member of the group becomes one of the six characters – Mr Birling, Mrs Birling, Sheila, Eric, Gerald Croft and Inspector Goole. The Inspector should ask the questions **as scripted** without spoken thoughts. The others answer by **speaking their thoughts** before giving the scripted answer.

For example: Mrs Birling: [thoughts spoken out loud – *how dare this man speak to me in that tone*] 'Yes, I think it was simply a piece of gross impertinence …'

### Character

The key characters and some words that can describe them:

| Arthur Birling (50s, wealthy mill owner) | Arrogant Overbearing Greedy |
| --- | --- |
| Sybil Birling (50s, Arthur Birling's wife) | Cold Unsympathetic Hypocrite |
| Sheila Birling (20s, their daughter) | Optimistic Sympathetic Naive |
| Eric Birling (20s, their son) | Alcoholic Spoilt Selfish |
| Gerald Croft (30 Sheila's fiancé) | Assured Narcissistic Remorseful |
| Inspector Goole (unreal ghostlike) | Probing Insistent Insightful |
| Edna (a servant) | Passive Servile |

### Creating impact in a production of *An Inspector Calls*

The main challenge for a modern director is to make the play relevant to a contemporary audience. On the one hand, it is arguable that society is very different today. On the other hand, there are important similarities. Priestley wanted his audience to examine the way people in society looked out for themselves without thinking about anybody else around them. Although the 21st century's global society is very different, inequality still remains. Examine the Inspector's final speech:

'There are millions and millions and millions of … (Eva Smiths) … left with us, with their lives, their hopes and fears, their suffering and a chance of happiness, all intertwined with our lives and what we think and say and do. We don't live alone. We are members of one body. We are responsible for each other.'

If you were to think about how the homeless, the poor or refugees fleeing war are struggling, you can see how the play could be relevant today.

Priestley was fascinated by mathematical theories of time. He believed that time was not experienced in a linear way and that we experience things simultaneously in our past, present and sometimes the future. Many of his plays were based on this belief, for example, *Time and the Conways*. The structure of *An Inspector Calls* is interesting and works with this theme. The action does not unfold on stage but is recreated from the memories of the characters. The audience builds a picture of these events, instead of having them played out directly on stage. In this way the impact is more psychological, with each audience member imagining the scenes involving Eva Smith.

## Activity ?

**Building tension**

Read from 'Oh, stop it both of you. And please remember' to the end of Act 2.

1 What can you learn from the stage directions? E.g. *rather agitated now* or *Shelia begins crying quietly.*

2 How might you use the stage space to reflect the atmosphere at this point in the play?

3 Consider how your voice can show emotion. Think about tone, emphasis, intonation and pause.

4 How can you build towards Eric's entrance?

5 Rehearse this scene and show it to others in your group.

## Activity ?

**Coup de theatre: a sudden dramatic change of events in a play**

In Act 3, the Birlings were relieved when it is discovered that the Inspector wasn't real and that no girl had died in the Infirmary that night. The final telephone call, announcing that a real inspector is on his way to ask questions about the suicide of a young girl, has a dramatic effect on the characters. This final moment of the play predicts the future, leaving the audience wondering how the family will deal with the visit of the **real** police inspector. It can be spine-tingling in the theatre.

1 Read the end of the play from *The telephone rings sharply* and note the stage directions: *There is a moment's complete silence. He puts the telephone down slowly and looks in a panic-stricken fashion at the others. As they stare guiltily and dumbfounded.*

2 How would you create these dramatic actions? Think about the use of silences, eye contact, and facial expression, as well as the spoken dialogue. Try it out with a group.

## Exam tip

Examiners will expect your answers to show the intended **impact** on the audience and the way your interpretation creates **meaning**. These exact words may not appear in the question.

# Section A Bringing texts to life

## Performing characters in *An Inspector Calls*

In the exam you will be asked to interpret an extract from the play. Some questions will cover your approach to playing a character, while others require you to comment on how a director would work with an actor to realise a performance, or how you would use design to enhance performance.

The Inspector himself adds drama: he controls the pace and tension by dealing with one line of enquiry at a time as the story of Eva's life is unravelled. He is a mysterious, ominous and unavoidable presence who seems to know what is going to happen before it does. Inspector Goole can be viewed as a conductor or puppeteer, orchestrating the action.

In the play there is a constant wrangling for high status and control. Both Mr Birling and Inspector Goole feel that they are the most important, as one is head of the household and the other has the authority of the law. Gerald also feels he has status because he is from a higher social class. Mrs Birling wants control of her home and children: she objects to being left out of conversations. Sheila and Eric are trying in very different ways to break free from the stifling atmosphere of the family and to assert their independence.

### Activity ?

**Playing Inspector Goole**

Read the Inspector's interrogation of Eric in Act 3 from 'When did you meet her again?' to 'What do you mean – not really?'

1   As an actor, how would you convey the Inspector's control in this scene? Refer to voice, movement and the use of the stage space.

2   How would you show the Inspector's different attitudes to Mr Birling and to Eric? You may refer to eye contact, pauses, gestures, and tone of voice or any other performance skills.

3   Annotate the text to indicate your ideas.

### Activity ?

**Playing status in a scene**

In a pair, read the exchange between Inspector Goole and Mr Birling in Act 1, shortly after the inspector arrives, from 'Inspector: Why?' to 'Birling: I told them'.

There is a power struggle between these two men – it is Birling's house and he is a renowned businessman, but Inspector Goole carries the authority of his office.

1   Who do you think has the higher status in the scene? How might the actor playing Birling play the scene to challenge the Inspector's authority? Discuss your ideas.

2   Now play the scene looking at different ways to show voice, eye contact, pause and movement. You could swap roles and play it again to see how it feels to receive as well as deliver the lines.

## Exam-style question

You are going to play Gerald. As a performer, explain two ways you would use physical skills to play the character in this extract. You must provide a reason for each suggestion.

The text below is only **part** of the extract. **(4 marks)**

## *An Inspector Calls* Act 1

**Inspector**: Now she had to try something else. So first she changed her name to Daisy Renton –

**Gerald**: (*startled.*) What?

**Inspector**: (*steadily*) said she changed her name to Daisy Renton.

**Gerald**: (*pulling himself together*) Do you mind if I give myself a drink, Sheila?

*Sheila merely nods, still staring at him, and he goes across to the sideboard for a whiskey*

**Inspector**: Where is your father, Miss Birling?

**Sheila**: He went into the drawing room, to tell my mother what was happening here. Eric, take the Inspector along to the drawing room.

*As Eric moves, the Inspector looks from Sheila to Gerald, then goes out with Eric*

Well Gerald?

**Gerald**: Well what, Sheila?

In answering this question, you might refer to the following:

**Gerald's startled facial expression** when the Inspector mentions Daisy Renton could show that he is shocked as he recognises the name. Plus, Gerald's attempts to avoid **eye contact by pouring himself a drink** with Sheila as he does not want her to notice his guilt. Gerald might use **deliberately casual movement** to walk across to the sideboard, where he **sits on a chair, legs crossed and leaning backwards calmly** sipping his drink, and is a good way to show that he aims to cover up his reaction.

## Working on the text as a director of *An Inspector Calls*

The exam questions will ask you to look at the extract from the viewpoint of a director. This will include the decisions made about an actor's performance and the director's ideas for design. The director of *An Inspector Calls* will need to make a decision whether to stage the play in a **naturalistic** setting or in a symbolic or **expressionist** style. Stephen Daldry's production for the National Theatre had an expressionist set. The Inspector was a symbolic figure travelling back from the 1940s to warn the Birlings about their lifestyle. Street people wearing 1940s clothes listened from the wasteland around the house but the Birlings and Gerald were costumed as in 1912. This concept reminded the audience that the 'confessions' were public not just private, and the 1940s costumes linked the play's Edwardian setting to the contemporary class divide to which Priestley wanted to draw attention.

## Exam tip

The question has asked for **two** examples with reasons for your ideas. The suggested responses refer to specific physical skills, with clear reasons why you would use them when playing the role of Gerald. There are 4 marks available so to get 2 marks for each physical skill you must also give your reason.

## Glossary

**Expressionist**: A style that expresses the inner world rather than recreating external reality. It uses symbolism, exaggeration and distortion.

**Naturalistic**: A style closely imitating real life.

## Activity ?

**Directing a scene**

In a group of five, read the scene in Act 1 from Inspector: 'If you come over here I'll show *you*' to Sheila's entrance after Inspector: 'Enquiries of this sort for instance'.

1  One student becomes the director. Play the scene without stopping. The director makes notes about voice, physicality and stage space. Discuss what was effective and which sections worked less well. Why?

2  What do the characters **want** in this scene? For example, Mr Birling wants to assert his authority and rebuke the Inspector. Play the scene with this focus. How did playing these intentions affect voice and movement?

3  The director now works on the scene with a focus on movement, gesture and facial expression, taking note of the stage directions, e.g. *Gerald and Eric exchange uneasy glances.* Include ideas from the actors. What worked well?

4  Now work on the scene again with a focus on voice. What are the different techniques for voice, e.g. pitch or intonation?

5  Discuss the work on this section and perform the scene again combining all your decisions. If possible, film the scene or show it to others. Evaluate your work.

## Designing for a production of *An Inspector Calls*

The play is in three acts but it only requires one set. The action of the play takes place on a single night in the dining room of the Birling's house, so there is no need for set changes. In the text Priestley describes in great detail the exact appearance of the room. His comments are intended to suggest how the set shows the audience the wealth these people have.

Ian MacNeil's set for Stephen Daldry's 1992 production of the play won many awards. The set design was expressionist, making it very clear to the audience that the play is not set in a naturalistic environment. The Birling's house is perilously balanced on stilts, high above a surrounding barren area. It could almost be from a horror film. At the end of the play the house collapses. Other designers have recreated the era with details such as a chandelier, fruit bowl, lamps and paintings.

## Taking it further

Research online or at the library for set designs for *An Inspector Calls* and compare the styles. Make notes on how designers have used colour, texture, shape, space and materials in their designs.

## Activity　?

**Analyse and compare the set designs**

1　How have the designers evoked mood and atmosphere?

2　How do the materials chosen suggest themes as well as location and historical context?

3　How do you think these designs might work in the play? Consider entrances and exits, use of stage space and how characters might use the space in key scenes.

## Lighting

Lighting creates mood and atmosphere in the theatre. It can also draw the audience's attention to important moments and convey things like the time of day or weather. *An Inspector Calls* takes place at night, so the lighting designer needs to create the impression of low light while ensuring that the audience can see. If a naturalist style is being followed, the designer would research the history of domestic lighting at the time, study the lighting implications of the text and consider the director's concept.

Priestley describes the lighting as the play opens as *'pink and intimate until the Inspector arrives, and then it should be brighter and harder'.* Lighting suggests the mood, which initially is comfortable, calm and relaxed. Once the Inspector begins his questioning, the mood changes, as people become edgy, angry, resentful and distressed. Naturalistic lighting does not make bold statements but there can be subtle changes that are barely noticeable to the audience, which change the atmosphere. The 'pink' of Priestley's directions implies soft lighting to create the mood for the celebratory dinner. The designer would decide where this light was coming from – candles on the table, lamps on sideboards or a chandelier? There are other occasions where stage directions or dialogue indicate light sources: when he shows Sheila the photograph the Inspector *'moves nearer a light – perhaps a standard lamp'.* This suggests that the room is dimly lit, which in turn creates atmosphere.

### Taking it further　◥

To find out about the lighting sources in 1912 do an internet search for 'Country Life history of domestic lighting'. Read the article on the history of domestic lighting in different periods. What else can you find out?

## Activity　?

**Look for lighting clues**

1　Examine the text from the viewpoint of a designer or director. Note the lighting states that are specifically scripted and those that are implied.

2　Select one section and plan in detail how the lighting would be used in the scene. Make sure you use **technical terms** to explain how the ideas would work in practice.

Below is a costume design for Sybil Birling. What does it tell you about her character?

Costume sketch for Sybil Birling by Mike Lees for Little Theatre, Leicester.

## Costumes

Costumes for *An Inspector Calls* can tell the audience about the characters as well as the historical period in which it is set. The play opens at the Birling's dinner party, which is a good opportunity to show the wealth and class of the family. Consideration will be given to the texture and fabrics used in the costumes. The Inspector, by comparison, appears plain. As the action progresses and characters leave the room, become anxious and distressed or leave the house, the costumes may change subtly to show the passage of time. In one production, Sheila had two identical dresses, one of which was broken down to convey her becoming dishevelled.

## Sound

Sound design creates real sounds, such as the telephone ring at the end of the play, but the designer might add other sounds or music to enhance the mood. There are few scripted sound effects, mainly doors slamming off stage or a doorbell ring, yet the sound can have a dramatic effect. The doorbell indicating the arrival of the Inspector rings *sharply*, interrupting Birling's smug speech and marking a connection between the Inspector's arrival and Birling's capitalist views.

## Activity

**Sound and music: heightening the atmosphere**

Copy out and complete the table to show four ways in which you might use music or sounds, other than those indicated in the text, to intensify or highlight the mood. The first example is done for you.

| Act | Description of music or sounds and what this indicates |
|---|---|
| Opening of Act 1 | A piano plays to suggest an elegant, relaxed atmosphere and to indicate the era. |
|  |  |
|  |  |
|  |  |
|  |  |

## *The Crucible* by Arthur Miller

### Performance context

When Arthur Miller's drama *The Crucible* first opened on Broadway in 1953, the USA was in a panic about the rise of communism. The first performance of *The Crucible* was on 2nd January 1953 at the Martin Beck Theatre on Broadway, New York. The set, designed by Boris Aronson, created a space with roughly chopped wooden walls and a sloped ceiling with a window and one door. Within this space the different settings could be created with stage furniture and properties. The setting was stylised and Arthur Miller commented that it was 'too cold' and barren. The stage was a proscenium arch with the audience seated in tiered rows in the auditorium. Miller describes his inspiration for *The Crucible* as 'what was in the air' in the USA. He saw a connection between the hysteria of the Salem witch trials and the hunt for communist activists. In the 1950s the USA was extremely concerned about the threat of communism, which was growing in Eastern Europe and China. A young senator named Joseph McCarthy carried out a campaign to root out communists in American public life. The hunt was known to be difficult for writers and entertainers, many of whom were labelled as communist sympathisers and were unable to continue working. Miller himself was accused and questioned.

A reconstruction of George Jacobs' trial by T.H. Matteson.

### Historical context

The American playwright Arthur Miller wrote *The Crucible* in 1953 about the 1692 witch trials in Salem, Massachusetts. Salem was a small, strictly Christian Puritan community: their religion forbade dancing and any form of decoration on clothing or in the home. Attending church every Sunday was very important and anyone who was missing had to answer to the minister. Life in Salem was hard: food was scarce and they feared that Native American tribes might attack them. In 1692, 200 people were accused of witchcraft and 20 were hanged. The Puritans believed in the Devil and thought that he could give certain humans the power to harm others. There were simmering tensions in Salem and resentment towards neighbours. Against this background a group of girls, led by Abigail Williams, were able to convince both the community leaders and the trial judges that there were witches in Salem.

---

### Taking it further

Find out more about what happened in Salem.

Read about Miller's visit to Salem in *Timebends* by Arthur Miller, pages 335–342.

### Exam tip

In the play the character Tituba says 'the Devil got him numerous witches'. Although the play is set in the 17th century, it was written in the 1950s. During the 1950s in the USA, there was a strong campaign against communists known as McCarthyism. This affected a lot of writers within the theatre and film industries. Quotes in the play such as the one above are really talking about the 'witch hunt' against communists in the 1950s.

In your exam you will need to show an understanding of the context of the play, so you might like to keep a list of quotes like this to help you.

### Taking it further

Research McCarthyism in 1950s USA on the History in an Hour website or in a book from the library.

# Section A Bringing texts to life

**Activity** ?

**Create a scene**

In a group one person takes on the role of John Proctor. Now use the strategy **conscience alley** to explore the dilemma in John Proctor's mind as he decides whether to confess.

## Glossary

**Conscience alley**: A way to explore how a character is feeling when they have to make an important decision. It can be described as 'voices in the head'. The group forms two equal lines, with each side having opposing views. The central character walks slowly down the middle and as they pass each person speaks persuasively. At the end, the person who walked through comments on how they felt.

A feature of the questioning of those accused of having communist sympathies was demanding that they named others who were involved. There is a direct comparison between this and the events in Salem. In Act 1 Tituba asks 'Who came to you with the Devil? Two? Three? Four? How many?'

In the programme notes for *The Crucible* at the Old Vic in 2014, directed by Yael Farber, we are reminded of the many Muslims held without trial at Guantanamo Bay on insubstantial evidence: the power of *The Crucible's* message is as strong today as it was in 1953. The play was famously performed in Shanghai, China, in 1980, where it evoked the atmosphere of life under Mao; an era of allegations and forced confessions, and a complete lack of freedom in society. Miller said that he thought the job of the artist was to remind people of what they have chosen to forget.

## The story of *The Crucible*

### Act 1

A group of girls dance naked in the woods while creating spells with Tituba, a black servant. Disturbed and fearing punishment, some feign sickness. A strong fear of witches in 1692 causes rumours to spread that the girls have been bewitched. John Proctor, a farmer who had an affair with Abigail, visits and she tells him that it is a 'pretence'. Events escalate and a witch finder is summoned to Salem. Under close questioning, Tituba 'confesses' to being visited by the Devil. Abigail leads the girls in copying Tituba in naming many women who they had seen with the Devil.

### Act 2

A court is set up. Mary Warren, Elizabeth and John Proctor's servant, is now a witness in court. She tells Elizabeth how the girls scream and faint to show that the accused is afflicting them. The girls accuse women who they have reason to dislike. Abigail accuses Elizabeth but the charges are false and John fights to save his wife. Elizabeth is imprisoned but saved from hanging because she is pregnant.

### Act 3

John brings Mary to court to admit that the girls are faking their 'fits'. The girls, led by Abigail, deny it and in desperation John admits his adultery. Elizabeth, asked to confirm the story, denies the affair to save his name. Abigail now leads the girls in accusing Mary Warren of witchcraft; terrified, she accuses Proctor of afflicting her. Outraged and frustrated, he wildly shouts out that he has seen the Devil. He is imprisoned.

### Act 4

Those found guilty of witchcraft can avoid hanging by confessing. John is due to hang and attempts are made to persuade him to confess and save his life. John thinks of his wife and three children and chooses to sign a confession. Told that his confession will be nailed to the church, he tears it up and the play closes with Elizabeth's reaction to his death.

The key characters and some words that can describe them:

| John Proctor | Powerful Imposing Guilty |
|---|---|
| Abigail Williams | Devious Threatening |
| Reverend Parris | Bitter Afraid Stubborn |
| Elizabeth Proctor | Reserved Fragile Honest |
| Judge Danforth | Strong Respected Terrifying |
| Mary Warren | Anxious Nervous |
| Reverend Hale | Eager Scholarly Sincere |
| Tituba | Loyal Fearful Boisterous |
| Giles Corey | Elderly Quarrelsome Comical |
| Rebecca Nurse | Calm Dignified Devout |
| The Putnams | show how greed and envy drove the accusations |
| Mercy, Susanna and Betty | are the girls influenced by Abigail |
| Cheever, Francis Nurse and Herrick | are established men of Salem affected by the events |

## Creating impact in a production of *The Crucible*

The title of the play is significant. A 'crucible' is a melting pot in which metals are heated and changed but it can also mean a severe ordeal or test. In the play characters undergo extreme changes, suffer ordeals and their faith is tested. The title represents the play's central themes and meanings.

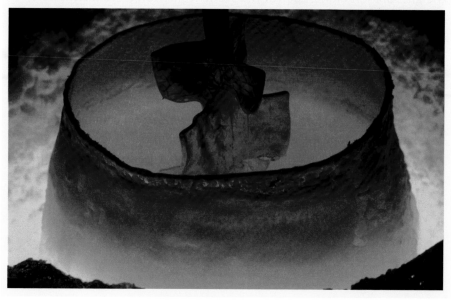

# Section A Bringing texts to life

The central idea in the play is how hysteria overpowered reason in Salem, fuelled by an undercurrent of fear and suspicion. As in 1950s USA during the McCarthy trials, friends turned against friends and divisions were created between partners. The rhythm of *The Crucible* has moments of quiet tension and others of hysterical climax.

Miller captures the hysteria of Salem in the climatic scenes of the play. In a production it is important that these moments contrast with quieter scenes and build to the climax. One of the most memorable scenes in the play comes towards the end of Act 3. The tense questioning of Elizabeth by Judge Danforth is underpinned by dramatic irony, as the audience know that John has confessed to adultery. The scene explodes into hysteria when Reverend Hale suggests that Abigail has 'always struck me false!' Directors and actors must decide what the high point of each scene will be and consider how to build the atmosphere.

## Working on the text as an actor in *The Crucible*

In your exam you will be asked to interpret an extract from the play. Some questions will concern your approach to playing a character, some will ask you to think from the point of view of a designer and some will require you to comment on how a director would work with an actor to realise a performance.

Abigail is a central character who drives the narrative: it is she who initiates the activities in the woods that led to the witch hunt and her relationship with John Proctor proves to be his downfall.

## Working on the text as a director of *The Crucible*

The exam questions will ask you to look at the extract from the viewpoint of a director: this will include the decisions made about an actor's performance and the director's ideas for design. *The Crucible* has four different locations so the director must consider the mood and atmosphere and stage furniture, while enabling smooth transitions from one to the other

Ezekiel Cheever, the clerk of the court, has a minor but important role in the play. His most significant scene is when he arrives at the Proctor's house with a warrant for Elizabeth's arrest. This is a key turning point in the play. The director has an overview of the play and all the production elements.

In your exam you will be asked to make decisions about characterisation and describe how you would see the role performed in your production. Your answer should focus on voice, physicality, stage space and stage directions.

## Activity ?

### Directing Cheever in Act 2

Indicate the line using the first and last few words. An example is shown below:

| Director's notes for Ezekiel Cheever | | |
|---|---|---|
| Skill | Line | Director's Note |
| 1 Eye contact | 'Why it is … Herrick, it is a needle' | Stare at Proctor with a look of horror |
| 2 Gesture | | |
| 3 Movement | | |
| 4 Voice | | |
| 5 Stage space | | |

> **Top tip**
>
> Use a chart like this to practise your approach to directing actors in other sections of the play.

## Activity ?

### Locations in *The Crucible*

Copy and complete the table below from the viewpoint of a director. Think about atmosphere and mood as well as the essential stage furniture. For example, Act 1 must have a bed for Betty. This has been filled in for you but you can add other stage furniture.

| | Location | Mood/atmosphere | Stage furniture |
|---|---|---|---|
| Act 1 | Bedroom in Parris' house | | Bed |
| Act 2 | | | |
| Act 3 | | | |
| Act 4 | | | |

> **Exam tip**
>
> In your exam you will be asked to make decisions about characterisation and describe how you would see the role performed in your production. Your answer should focus on voice, physicality, stage space and stage directions.

*The Crucible* Act 1: The bed is placed downstage to show its importance in this Act. There is one simple chair. The entrance to the room is suggested by a free-standing door frame. Lighting creates the atmosphere.

## Activity ?

**Directing Mary Warren in Act 2**

In a group of three, read the closing scene from 'Mr Proctor very likely' to the end of the Act.

1   Choose someone to take the role of director. The rest of the group act out the scene without stopping, while the director makes notes about voice, physicality and stage space. Discuss what was effective and which sections worked less well. Why?

2   What do the characters want in this scene? Proctor wants Mary to tell the court that Abigail is lying and Mary wants to save herself from Abigail's vengeance. Play the scene with this focus. How did playing the intentions affect voice and movement?

3   The director now works on the scene with a focus on movement, gesture and facial expression, taking note of the stage directions, e.g. *moving menacingly towards her*. Include ideas from the actors. What worked well?

4   Now work on the scene again with a focus on voice. What are the different techniques for voice, e.g. pitch?

5   Discuss your work on this section and perform the scene again combining all your decisions. If possible, film the scene or show it to others. Evaluate your work.

## Designing for a production of *The Crucible*

Look at the image of the set design below for *The Crucible* from the Old Vic production in London in 2014.

The play was performed in-the-round with seats on the stage, giving the feeling that the audience were complicit in the accusations. The atmosphere was bleak and gloomy. The ornate balconies were covered with dirty grey fabric, which continued over rusting iron towers at the rear. These towers contained broken windowpanes and the floor was dark grey stone. The play opened with the smell of herbs, suggesting the lingering aroma of Tituba's potions. The actors carried simple items of furniture such as a bed, a chair or a table, on and off stage, positioning them to suggest the locations.

Set design for The Crucible at the Old Vic Theatre.

**Taking it further**

Look online or at the library for set designs for *The Crucible*. Make notes on how designers have used colour, texture, shape, space and materials in their designs.

### Costume

It is important when considering costume for *The Crucible* to ensure that they reflect Puritan values. Nothing is decorated, women covered their heads, and farmers and poorer people would wear simple garments made from rough fabrics. Higher-status characters would wear richer fabrics but would obey Puritan rules. A director would work with the designer to reflect the play's concept through costume as well as set design. For example, the Old Vic production above dressed the girls in dull green, grey and navy dresses that looked shapeless and homemade. The higher-status men, such as Putnam, wore black, well-cut jackets and breeches. Shoes also showed status: Tituba often had bare feet; the poorer women wore scruffy brown boots.

**Activity** **?**

**Analyse this design**

- How has the designer evoked mood and atmosphere?
- How do the materials chosen suggest themes as well as location and historical context?
- How do you think this design might work in the play? Consider entrances and exits, use of stage space and how characters might use the space in key scenes.

**Activity** **?**

**Design the costumes for a production**

Working as a group discuss the concept of your production, then choose one character each.

Research the style, shape and texture of the costume that your character would wear in one scene of the play.

Create a Pinterest page for the group, saving images and ideas for your character. These pins can come from theatre productions or from historical research.

# Section A Bringing texts to life

## Activity ?

**Lighting designer's notes for Act 4**

Act 4 is set in the jail. The scene begins in darkness and the sun rises during the act.

Examine the text from the viewpoint of the lighting designer. Look at the designers' notes below and write your own notes for the lighting of this Act in the same style.

## Lighting

Lighting can create mood, heighten tension and indicate location. In the Old Vic production discussed earlier, the upstairs room of the house in Act 1 was suggested by a trapdoor in the stage with a flight of stairs going down. When open, this was lit by a shaft of golden light indicating activity downstairs. If you examine the text you will be able to see where essential light is suggested by stage directions or where it is implied in the dialogue. Artistic lighting decisions can be added to enhance atmosphere or create mood.

A lighting designer's analysis of Act 2 indicates there is a fire and when Proctor opens the door he says 'the smell of nightfall', suggesting the setting sun. There was no electricity in 1692 so the room would be lit with candles, which cast shadows. Others come to the house: it is dark so they may arrive with lanterns. At the end of the act Proctor 'walks as though towards a great horror, facing the open sky'. This implies non-naturalistic lighting as a climax, probably the interval.

Below are initial notes made by a designer.

## Designer's notes

*Act 2*

*Opens with a single candle burning on the table. Light permeates, Shadows. Fire flickers shadows dance on the walls, Corners dark. Elizabeth's face lit by firelight as she stirs pot. Proctor enters and darkening skies are seen. Glimpse of low sun behind moody clouds. Proctor lights another candle when he complains that 'it is winter in here yet'. The community is fearful without light. Proctor stands outside – a low red sunset – threatening not pretty. Moonlight through windows – shadows. Cheever and Herrick bring lanterns – room brightens. Elizabeth exits and the lanterns taken and room plunged into gloom, single candle on table – fire almost out. Final moments non-naturalistic shaft of white light on Mary Warren on the floor. Proctor back to audience in doorway. Black clouds obscure a hazy moon*

## Taking it further

Find out how sound designers work with directors.

Explore the ways that sound is created in the theatre.

Find out more about how sound has been used in modern productions of *The Crucible*.

## Sound

Sound design is similar to lighting in that it is used for realistic sound, e.g. the clanking of chains as well as creating mood and atmosphere. In Act 1 sound establishes the angry crowd of villagers in the room below Betty's bedroom, and in Act 2 the audience hears the creaking wagon and horses taking Elizabeth to prison. In both of these cases the sound is real but it also has an emotional effect: the crowd is intimidating for Parris and the departing wagon exposes the horror of Elizabeth's situation.

A director and sound designer might also include sound that is not necessarily scripted by the playwright, to heighten tension or evoke an emotional response from the audience. For example, a long discordant violin note at the end of Act 2, accompanying Mary Warren's final cries of 'I cannot', builds tension.

## *Government Inspector* by Nikolai Gogol in a version by David Harrower

### Performance context

*The Government Inspector* is a political comedy written by Russian playwright Nikolai Gogol in 1836. It satirises corrupt bureaucracy under Tsar Nicholas I. During that time, the Russian Empire was torn between wanting modernisation and keeping traditional values, and Gogol's play reflects this conflict. It is set in a small town where corruption is widespread. Gogol's 1836 play was translated into English by Arthur Sykes in 1842. Modern translations tend to use the job titles of the officials and have updated references to the civil service, dropping all Russian words and family naming traditions. David Harrower's version is titled *Government Inspector* and it was first performed at The Young Vic Theatre in London. The chaotic atmosphere of the office of the Mayor in the opening scene immediately shows the town's officials as ridiculously inefficient and unprofessional, despite the large number of them who have official government titles. A self-indulgent young man, Khlestakov, in an absurd case of mistaken identity, is thought to be a government inspector who has come to examine the way the town is run and managed. Harrower's adaptation makes the play fitting for contemporary British society with jokes that an audience recognises: for example, about the cleanliness of hospitals, high-ranking officials taking bribes and attitudes towards teachers. The fact that Khlestakov, a minor clerk, is able to pose as a high-status public official demonstrates the ignorance of the Mayor and his officials, who are themselves completely corrupt. The judge is easily bribed, the postmaster steams open letters, while the police are drunk and brawling. The most corrupt of all is the Mayor who takes bribes, squanders money allotted to the building of a church and takes money from local shopkeepers. The lack of communication between the town and the officials in Saint Petersburg highlights how the Russian government was incapable of managing the majority of the country. In satirising small-town corruption Gogol also tackled the theme of human corruption, and Harrower's version of the play makes this very relevant to the 21st century.

### Taking it further

Carry out some research to find out more about how Tsar Nicholas I governed Russia and how this affected the people. Look for information about the class structure, which was strictly enforced. It consisted of four levels – the clergy, nobility, urbanites and rural dwellers (essentially peasants).

### The story of *Government Inspector*

#### Act 1

The play begins in the Mayor's house where he has called a meeting with the town's leading officials, including the judge, the superintendent of schools, the director of charities, the town doctor and a local police officer. The Mayor informs them that a government inspector is due to arrive from Saint Petersburg. In a panic, he tells his officials to cover up all the corruption in the town. Bobchinsky and Dobchinsky, two local landowners, rush in with news that they have seen the government inspector staying at the local inn. The Mayor sets off to meet him at the inn. The Mayor's wife, Anna, and daughter, Maria, are very excited about the arrival of the inspector.

#### Act 2

In Khlestakov's shabby room at the inn his servant, Osip, reveals that his master is a clerk of a very low rank, who has lost all his money gambling and can't pay his bill. Osip is sent to persuade the kitchen staff, who have been ordered not to serve Khlestakov, to provide a meal for his master. The Mayor arrives, believing that Khlestakov is the expected government inspector, and offers to show him the town's institutions – the hospital, schools and the prison. Khlestakov thinks he is being arrested for not paying his bill! The Mayor invites 'the inspector' to stay at his home, and Khlestakov accepts this offer without knowing that he is being mistaken for someone else.

*Government Inspector.* Which character do you think each of these actors is playing?

### Act 3

At the Mayor's home his wife and daughter are eagerly awaiting the arrival of the government inspector. Khlestakov and the Mayor arrive after a tour of the hospital and a hearty meal. Khlestakov realises that he is being mistaken for a high-ranking government official and tells of his luxurious life in Saint Petersburg. When he goes to his room, the Mayor's wife and daughter argue over which of them Khlestakov liked the most.

### Act 4

The Mayor and his officials plan to bribe the government inspector to prevent him from reporting them to the officials in Saint Petersburg. Each official visits Khlestakov's room, giving him the increasingly extravagant amounts of money he requests 'as a loan'. Amused by the whole situation, Khlestakov writes to his friend, a Saint Petersburg newspaper columnist. A group of local shopkeepers arrive to plead with 'the inspector' to listen to their complaints about the corruption and bribery in the town. In a farcical scene, Khlestakov begins to seduce Maria when Anna enters, blaming her daughter for 'disgusting' behaviour. Maria leaves in tears and Khlestakov immediately declares his love for Anna! Maria walks in on them whereupon Khlestakov asks Maria to marry him. The Mayor and his wife are delighted and willingly give their consent. Osip, meanwhile, has made plans for Khlestakov to leave the town before his deception is discovered. Khlestakov tells them that he is leaving town for only a few days and will return soon to marry Maria.

## Act 5

The Mayor and his wife boast of the privileged life they will lead in Saint Petersburg once their daughter has married this high-ranking official. The postmaster arrives, having steamed open Khlestakov's letter, to tell them about the deception. The Mayor is unwilling to believe this story but slowly realises that he has been tricked. A policeman arrives with a letter informing them that a government inspector has arrived from Saint Petersburg and that they are to report immediately to the inn.

At the end of the play Gogol suggested a *'tableau of consternation'* lasting several minutes, where the characters absorb the news that the 'inspector' who they had bribed was a fraud and that a real government inspector had just arrived.

## Characters

The director's ideas for the play will determine how the actors approach their roles. This means that the performances will differ from one production to another. Gogol's original script is full of wordplay, much of which doesn't translate into English very well. He gives his characters amusing names that evoke something of their character. Lyapkin-Tyapkin implies 'slapdash' and in one translation he is known as 'Judge Slappencatchit', Khlopov, the schools superintendent, is derived from the Russian verb meaning 'a dull thud' and Zemlyanika means 'strawberry', perhaps suggesting that the trustee of charitable institutions is sweet and easily squashed.

Key characters and some words that can describe them:

| The Mayor | Paranoid  Obsequious  Dishonest |
| --- | --- |
| Khlestakov | Irresponsible  Selfish  Immoral |
| Anna | Self-centered  Inquisitive  Haughty |
| Maria | Flirtatious   Trusting  Unsophisticated |
| Osip | Shrewd  Cunning  Loyal |
| Lyapkin-Tyapkin | Pompous  Old-fashioned  Honorable |
| Zemlyanika | Officious  Interfering  Fussy |
| Khlopov | Fearful  Troubled  Indecisive |

## Creating impact in a production of *Government Inspector*

Harrower's *Government Inspector* is a fast-paced comedy with elements of **farce** and **slapstick**. The impact on the audience, therefore, is most likely to be to make them laugh. Gogol's intention for the original play was essentially to provoke thought, as he wanted to expose the widespread corruption in the Tsar's government. He was distressed when audiences described the play as satirical comedy. David Harrower's version combines both these aspects: it is employs physical and verbal comedy while satirising vain ambition and bureaucratic incompetence.

**Activity**   ?

Divide into groups and create a frozen image for the end of the play that shows the shock and disbelief of the characters. Think about facial expression and physicality – imagine what your characters are thinking. Now add the emotions of the characters by speaking their thoughts aloud one at a time.

**Activity**   ?

Work in a group. Choose one of the 'unseen' events from the list below.

1  Khlestakov is unable to pay his bill, so he and Osip are moved to a shabby room at the inn and informed that they will not be served any more meals until the bill is paid.

2  Khlestakov tours the 'newly improved' hospital with the Mayor.

3  The shopkeepers meet to plan what they will say in their appeal to the 'government inspector'.

Read the scene in the play where the event is discussed or described and then improvise the scene.

**Glossary**

**Farce**: A style of comedy that involves improbable situations and physical humour.

**Slapstick**: This style of comedy involves exaggerated characters and boisterous action, for example, falling over or throwing custard pies.

# Section A Bringing texts to life

## Activity ?

In Act 2, Scene 4, Khlestakov is served a very poor meal by an unwilling waiter. The comedic impact is created partly by the actor's movement, facial expression and vocal intonation, but also through use of props. There are three characters – Khlestakov, Osip and the waiter.

1   Read the scene and note how the comedy might be created, both physical and vocal. Osip has few lines in this scene but his role is important. Why?

2   Improvise a scene in a modern setting – a restaurant, pub or café – where a waiter serves a meal to Khlestakov who, although he is very hungry, complains about the quality. Include Osip and think about how he interacts with the other two characters.

3   Now return to the text and play the scripted scene, incorporating the physical and vocal humour from your improvisation.

## Glossary

**Dramatic irony**: This occurs when the audience knows something that the characters do not; this puts the audience at an advantage over the characters and makes them more involved.

**Aside**: This is a remark made by a character to the audience that is not heard by the other characters on stage. This was popular in Elizabethan and Restoration theatre.

## Taking it further

There are similarities between this scene and a hilarious scene in the farcical comedy *One Man, Two Guvnors* by Richard Bean, involving the central character, played by James Corden, simultaneously serving a meal to his two masters. Find out more about this production, staged at the National Theatre in 2011.

## Working as an actor in a production of *Government Inspector*

In your exam you will be asked to interpret an extract from the play. Some questions will concern your approach to playing a character, some will ask you to think from the point of view of a designer and some will require you to comment on how a director would work with an actor to realise a performance.

Act 2, Scene 4 is a subtle comic examination of corruption. The Mayor openly bribes the 'government inspector' and Khlestakov gradually realises that he has been mistaken for an extremely important person. The audience know that he is a poverty stricken clerk who has gambled away all his money; the comedy here depends on **dramatic irony** and employs **asides** where the Mayor speaks directly to the audience.

## Exam-style question

Read the scene from Mayor: 'If you're a little short of funds' to 'Really very rare'. You are going to play the Mayor. He is a very important character in the play.

As a performer give three suggestions of how you would use performance skills to engage the audience in this extract. You must provide a reason for each suggestion. **(6 marks)**

Your answer could include the following points.

Using attentive movement and gesture, such as wringing hands and leaning towards Khlestakov when you offer him 'funds'. This lowers the Mayor's status in front of 'His Excellency', playing on the dramatic irony and mistaken identity to engage the audience.

When speaking the asides to the audience, employ a sarcastic vocal tone in sharp contrast to the flattering voice, moving away from the action to a point very close to the audience, and speaking directly to individuals. The audience will feel part of the action, yet superior, as they know that Khlestakov is merely a clerk.

When asking Khlestakov to stay at your house, use an obviously insincere vocal tone and exaggerated movements and gestures. For example, walking away with flamboyant hand gestures on 'I wonder, would… No, No' and 'I was going to ask if – but no no. No, I can't. I can't'. This ridiculous grovelling will amuse the audience, who know the true situation. The line 'I hate obsequiousness and fawning and all that…' coming almost immediately afterwards, will have even more impact.

## Exam tip

Read the question carefully. This question asks you to make **three points** about **performance skills** and to give **reasons** for your choices. Always make the exact number of points required by the question – not fewer and not more. Make sure you give clear reasons for your suggestions. This section outlined in the exam question is similar in length to the extract that will be on your exam paper.

## Working on the text as a director of *Government Inspector*

The exam question will ask you to look at the extract from the viewpoint of a director – this will include the decisions made about the overall concept, an actor's performance and the director's ideas for design. The play is a fast-paced comedy, sharply satirical with farcical movements and plot lines. There are frequent long monologues from the Mayor and Khlestakov, which provide a challenge for both actors and the director. The play's structure gains pace with 11 short scenes in Act 4. The director must ensure that the pace of the play is swift while the complex story is clearly told.

Act 3, Scene 4 includes a range of comic opportunities. Anna and Khlestakov are pretending to be more important and sophisticated than they actually are. Anna uses French words to appear cultured, whereas Khlestakov tells elaborate stories that make him sound inspirational and important. Farcical and slapstick comedy occur when Khlestakov teases the assembled officials, making them sit and stand to order and also, towards the end of the scene, when he falls and is caught. Khlestakov's implication that he has a close friendship with writers such as **Pushkin** – 'How's it going Pushky?' – will also amuse the audience, who will recognise the absurdity of his claims.

### Glossary

**Alexander Pushkin**: A famous Russian poet who was held in the same high esteem in Russia as Shakespeare is in England. He was killed in a duel in 1837, a year after Gogol's original play was written. Pushkin, who was a friend of Gogol, told him the story on which *Government Inspector* is based.

In this photograph from a production at Perth Theatre, Scotland (2011), you can see the director's use of farcical humour. Notice the facial expressions of the actors.

## Activity ?

Read Act 3, Scene 4 and consider how you would direct the actor playing Khlestakov to engage the audience in the comedy. Make notes about physicality, voice and the use of the stage space. You may prefer to create a visual map of your ideas.

Similarly, Khlestakov's list of publications in Harrower's version includes well-known titles, such as *Alice in Wonderland*. Gogol listed similarly popular works that the Russian audience would recognise and find comical. The scene could be rather static, as the Mayor, his family and officials listen to Khlestakov's long speeches with little opportunity for movement. The humour arises from verbal comedy, the reactions of those listening and moments of slapstick.

## Designing for a production of *Government Inspector*

The designers of set and costume, together with the director, will consider the era in which the play is set, in this case 1836, and decide whether the production will be authentically historical, or set in a modern context. The set design must suggest several locations and could be stylised or naturalistic. The majority of the play is set in the Mayor's house with Act 2 in Khlestakov's shabby room at the local inn, and Act 4, Scene 2 taking place in Khlestakov's '*salon jaune*'.

Northern Broadsides' 2012 production of *Government Inspector* was set in a contemporary Pennine town with a live brass band. The production explored the greed and small town corruption of the Councillors and the costumes included a loud, checked suit for Khlestakov (who was renamed Snapper). The Young Vic's production of Harrower's *Government Inspector* kept the overall style of 19th-century Russia but added an anarchic twist. Look at the photograph and note how the Russian 19th-century fashion has been adapted in an almost pantomimic style.

## Taking it further

Look on the internet for photographs of the Young Vic and Northern Broadside productions.

Find out about the director and designers' concept. What do you think the set and costume designs suggested to the audience?

Young Vic production.

## Activity ?

Work with a small group or in a pair.

1 Discuss how you would stage the play: would you set it in a modern context?

2 What type of stage would you choose – thrust, proscenium arch, traverse or in-the-round?

3 Think about the style of the furniture, the colours and the fabrics that you would choose.

4 How would the actors use the stage furniture?

5 What are your reasons for these choices?

6 How would you stage the play to realise a swift transition between Acts 1 and 2 and between Act 4, Scenes 1 and 2?

Create a **collage** or **mood board** of all your ideas. Include images of furnishings and objects that might dress the set, e.g. lamps, cushions, plants or paintings and if possible, add snippets of fabric.

## Costume

Costume can locate the play in its time period for the audience, suggest weather and time of day. The **costume designer** will also need to reflect character in the designs. For example, Anna is vain and wants to attract Khlestakov's attention. She might wear a red dress decorated with jewels with a neckline cut as low as possible for the period. The Mayor is corrupt and swindles the shopkeepers so will probably be better dressed than Zemlyanika or Khlopov. The costume also reflects the mood of the play. Therefore, as *Government Inspector* is a farce, one possible idea would be for characters to wear bright colours. The ragged figure in bandages, who appears at the end of Act 4, Scene 10, is a serious reminder of the effect that the corruption has on ordinary citizens. The costume will have a visual impact on the audience.

## Sound

Sound design for *Government Inspector* would create essential scripted effects, such as the clamour of the shopkeepers' protest in the street, as well as music or incidental sounds to add to the atmosphere. The moment when the hands appear at the windows is accompanied by shouts from the street; this could have a haunting effect on the audience.

## Lighting

Lighting will enhance the mood or atmosphere in addition to suggesting location. The lighting will link to the director's desired mood and atmosphere. Lighting for Act 2 will need to create the gloom of the shabby inn, while the Mayor's house is lavish and there may be chandeliers to suggest his wealth. The '*salon jaune*' is clearly a special room so lighting will mirror this mood. When the crowds reach to the windows and the ragged figure appears, the lighting designer might mark this mood with a subtle lighting change.

### Taking it further

Find images of productions of *Government Inspector*. Recent productions have been staged by: Birmingham Repertory Theatre directed by Roxana Silbert, The Young Vic directed by David Farr and Northern Broadsides directed by Conrad Nelson. Look carefully at how lighting adds to the mood of the scene. How do you think these effects have been created?

# Section A Bringing texts to life

## Taking it further

Look at the Shakespeare's Globe website for information about the reconstructed Globe in London.

## Twelfth Night by William Shakespeare

### Historical context

*Twelfth Night*, believed to be completed around 1601, towards the end of the reign of Queen Elizabeth I (1558–1603), reflects the uncertainty of this significant historical moment. It was written as entertainment for the end of the Christmas season and early performances took place in Middle Temple Hall in London. In later years, Shakespeare's plays were presented in the original Globe Theatre. A reconstruction of this theatre now stands on the South Bank in London. The plot of *Twelfth Night* revolves around a central female character, who is pretending to be a man. This is interesting because in Shakespeare's theatre there were no female players. The female roles were played by boys whose voices had not yet broken. Therefore, in *Twelfth Night*, a boy would be playing a girl who is pretending to be a man! The audience would have enjoyed the ensuing confusion. The Globe stage thrust out into the audience where the 'groundlings' stood. More expensive covered seats were in the galleries. Shakespeare's comedies always had a happy ending, often involving marriages.

### The story of *Twelfth Night*

#### Act 1

A love triangle and mistaken identity are the key elements of the plot. Duke Orsino is in love with Lady Olivia and he wants to persuade her to marry him but Olivia, grieving for her dead brother, rejects his advances. Meanwhile, a young noblewoman called Viola has been shipwrecked on the island and believes that her brother, Sebastian, has drowned. The ship's captain tells Viola about Orsino and Olivia. Viola says she wishes to go and work in Olivia's home. She disguises herself as a man, called Cesario. Orsino employs Cesario as a page and gives him the task of courting Olivia on his behalf. Olivia falls in love with Cesario without knowing that 'he' is a woman.

We meet Olivia's uncle, Sir Toby Belch, Olivia's maid Maria and Sir Andrew Aguecheek. Belch pretends to help the wealthy Aguecheek win Olivia's hand in marriage only so that Aguecheek will pay for his drinking.

#### Act 2

We learn that Viola's twin has been rescued from the sea by a sea captain Antonio. While Malvolio, Olivia's pompous steward, annoys Aguecheek, Belch and Feste (Olivia's professional fool) by reprimanding them for their raucousness following a night out. As revenge they and Fabian decide to play a trick on him. Maria, Olivia's quick-witted maid, writes a letter as if from Olivia, expressing her love for Malvolio. He believes the letter is from Olivia.

#### Act 3

Sir Andrew Aguecheek, who is also trying to court Olivia, is jealous and challenges Cesario to a duel. Antonio arrives, mistakes Cesario (Viola) for her twin brother Sebastian and defends him. Viola realises that Antonio may have seen her brother but leaves before Sebastian arrives.

Malvolio appears, dressed in ridiculous clothing as instructed to within the love letter. Olivia finds Malvolio's behaviour to be very strange and is convinced that he is mad. Sir Toby Belch locks him in a dark room as punishment.

## Act 4

Aguecheek, mistaking Sebastian for Cesario, hits him. Sir Toby Belch steps into the fight and draws his sword against Sebastian. Olivia intercedes and sends everyone away, still thinking that Sebastian is Cesario. Olivia and Sebastian fall in love, Olivia sends for a priest and they are married.

## Act 5

Orsino and Viola (still disguised as Cesario) come to Olivia's where they meet again with Antonio. Antonio, believing Cesario is Sebastian, accuses her of being ungrateful. Olivia arrives and announces that she has just married Cesario. Aguecheek complains about being hit by her. The confusion ends when Sebastian enters and Viola reveals her true identity. Orsino realises he has been in love with Viola all along, and she agrees to marry him. Sir Toby Belch and Maria also decide upon a wedding. Everyone is happy apart from Malvolio who leaves muttering, 'I'll be revenged on the whole pack of you'.

Olivia (Amanda Drew) and Viola (Rebecca Hall). The National Theatre 2011.

### Activity ?

**Mistaken identity**

Make a diagram showing where in the play characters are mistaken for someone else, the reasons and the consequences. You should include:

- trickery, such as Maria's forged letter
- deliberate pretence – Viola's disguise as Cesario
- confusion between the twins Viola and Sebastian.

Your diagram can include images, quotations and charts.

## Character

In Shakespeare's theatre the audience could easily identify 'stock' characters in the play, such as the romantic hero (Orsino), the clown (Feste), the heroine (Viola) and the loyal servant (Maria). In contemporary productions directors will look for parallels in modern society.

The chart on the next page is a good starting point for understanding the personalities of each character. Think about how the descriptions

# Section A Bringing texts to life

## Glossary

**Pathos**: Something that evokes a feeling of pity or sadness.

## Exam tip

Remember to use **specific vocabulary** when you write about voice or movement and give reasons why you have made these decisions. Always keep the intended effect on the **audience** at the centre of the answer.

suggested below might affect the voice and physicality used. For example, Malvolio is pompous, which implies that he has a high opinion of himself – his movement could reflect this trait by using an upright stance and confident use of eye contact. Sir Toby Belch has a larger-than-life personality, so he could move in a flamboyant manner. The actor playing Olivia may speak slowly in a low, soft voice when she is sorrowful, whereas the hot-headed Sir Andrew Aguecheek might speak loudly and harshly.

Key characters and some words that can describe them are listed here:

| Duke Orsino | Powerful  Sophisticated  Dreamy |
|---|---|
| Lady Olivia | Sorrowful  Passionate  Superior |
| Viola | Charming  Innocent  Witty |
| Malvolio | Pompous  Sycophantic  Ambitious |
| Sir Toby Belch | Irreverent  Playful  Reckless |
| Sir Andrew Aguecheek | Foolish  Prosperous  Hot-headed |
| Feste | Entertaining  Shrewd  Faithful |
| Sebastian | Honourable  Fearless  Caring |
| Maria | Loyal  Cunning  Mischievous |

### Creating impact in a production of *Twelfth Night*

*Twelfth Night* is a comedy. It does have some serious scenes and some **pathos**, but is predominantly a funny play. The desired impact on the audience will be to make them laugh. The slapstick comedy of Sir Toby Belch and Sir Andrew Aguecheek is signalled by prose and bawdy language, whereas Feste is a professional fool whose music, songs and jokes contribute to the festive spirit. The mistaken identity of Viola and Sebastian and the wordplay of the witty Viola give rise to subtler comedy.

## Activity ?

Read Act 2, Scene 3 from 'A love song, a love song' to 'She shall know of it by this hand'. Note: this section is a similar length to the printed extract on the exam paper.

1 Think about what Sir Toby, Aguecheek and Feste are doing. How might you create this raucous atmosphere? Try out your ideas in practice.

2 It is often hard to play a drunken character truthfully as it is easy to exaggerate too much. Use playing cards 2–10 (as before) to determine levels. If Sir Toby plays 2 he is sober but playing 10 he can hardly stand up. Which level is most effective?

3 How angry is Maria? Again use the cards to explore the level. What happens when, for example, Maria is 8 and Sir Toby is 4? Which combination is the most amusing?

4 What is Maria's objective in this scene? How would she use her voice to discipline Sir Toby?

5 Where is the scene set? What do you think the house is like? How might it be furnished? What kind of props would contribute to the noise?

Richard Wilson as Malvolio at The Courtyard Theatre RSC (2009).

## Working as an actor on *Twelfth Night*

In your exam you will be asked to interpret an extract from the play. Some questions will concern your approach to playing a character, some will ask you to think from the point of view of a designer and some will require you to comment on how a director would work with an actor to realise a performance.

## Exam-style questions

Discuss these questions then plan answers, as a group, based on your practical work.

1  You are going to play Sir Toby Belch. Explain two ways you would use vocal skills to play this character in this extract.

2  You are going to play Maria. As a performer, give three suggestions of how you would use performance skills to show this role from her entrance to the end of the extract. You must provide a reason for each suggestion.

3  As a director, discuss how you would use staging, props or stage furniture to bring this extract to life for your audience. You should make reference to the context in which the text was created and performed. **(9 marks)**

### Activity ?

**Malvolio and the 'box tree' scene – Act 2, Scene 5**

In this scene, Malvolio reads the letter that Maria has forged. Sir Toby, Sir Andrew and Fabian hide in a box tree hedge to observe his reactions. Read the scene from 'Malvolio: *[sees the letter]* What employment have we here?' to 'I will do everything that thou wilt have me.' *[Exit]*

1  Work in a group of five, with one student taking on the role of director.

2  Think about the use of **stage furniture** – in this case the box tree. How can the positioning of the three observers be comic? They need to be seen by the audience, but not by Malvolio.

3  How would Malvolio use the **stage space**?

4  Explore the use of Malvolio's voice and movement. How could his voice and movement demonstrate his reaction to the letter?

5  How might the characters that are watching express their delight both vocally and with facial expression? Remember they cannot leave the hedge.

# Section A Bringing texts to life

## Taking it further

Watch Malvolio's 'cross gartered' scene in Tim Carroll's 2012 production, featuring Mark Rylance and Stephen Fry, by searching for 'Shakespeare: Twelfth Night (Shakespeare's Globe)' on YouTube.

## Activity ?

### Create a locations storyboard

There are **six** different settings in the play: Orsino's palace, a sea coast, Olivia's house, Olivia's garden, Malvolio's 'dark room' in the house and a street setting.

1  Imagine that you are designing the set – where would you set the play and in what era? What would be your desired effect on a modern audience?

2  Look through the play and note down the different locations and what happens in each space, e.g. Act 1, Scene 1: Orsino's Palace – Orsino pines for Olivia.

3  Find images that match your ideas for the set – include houses, furniture, lamps, rugs, windows, gardens, etc, suitable for your chosen concept. On a large sheet of paper or on Pinterest create a design storyboard by placing the images alongside the scene locations.

## Activity ?

Take a look at the costume drawings opposite. What do they tell you about the characters?

## Working on the text as a director of *Twelfth Night*

Directors usually have a concept for their production of a play: this might involve setting it in a different era or location to create meaning for an audience. Edward Hall's 2012 production for Propeller, an all-male theatre company, had a modern physical style using masks and contemporary costumes. Another all-male production was staged at Shakespeare's Globe in 2012 with Mark Rylance as Olivia and Stephen Fry as Malvolio. This production sought to be historically authentic in every detail. In addition to men playing all roles, the costumes were dyed using Elizabethan methods and faces were made up using traditional materials.

## Activity ?

### Mistaken identity

Read Act 4, Scene 1. Sebastian is mistaken for Cesario (Viola) and he is challenged to a duel.

1  One student becomes the director. Play the scene without stopping.

2  The director makes notes about **voice**, **physicality** and **stage space**. Discuss what was effective and which sections worked less well. Why?

3  What does each character **want** in this scene? For example, Sebastian wants to get away from them and Sir Toby wants to fight. Play the scene with this focus. How did playing these intentions affect voice and movement?

4  The director should now work on the scene with a focus on movement, gesture and facial expression, taking note of the **stage directions**, e.g. *restrains Sebastian, frees himself, draws his sword*. Think about how a director might work with the actors to amuse the audience.

## Designing for a production of *Twelfth Night*: set, lighting, sound and costume

Productions at the original Shakespeare's Globe Theatre would have been presented on a bare thrust stage in the afternoon. There was no electricity for lighting and sound effects. Actors carried torches to signify night and candles were burnt to suggest indoor evening settings. The pillars that supported the Globe's canopy would probably have represented the hedges. In modern productions, designers, working with the director, will design the space to meet the needs of the concept and the requirements of the locations. For example, director Lucy Bailey and her designer Katrina Lindsay set her Manchester Royal Exchange production in a hotel.

## Costumes

Costumes locate the play in its period for the audience. Costumes can also reflect character, add status, suggest weather and time of day and, on occasions, become significant to the plot. In *Twelfth Night* costume is important because there is disguise and mistaken identity. Viola dresses as a man and looks identical to Sebastian. Feste disguises himself as Sir Topas (a fictional clergyman). While Malvolio's yellow cross-gartered stockings provide one of the key comic scenes. The costume designer will work closely with the director to reflect the themes. The same designer would normally design both the set and the costumes.

## Lighting

Lighting creates mood and atmosphere in the theatre. It can also draw the audience's attention to important moments and convey the time of day or weather. Lighting and sound could be used to create the storms at sea in *Twelfth Night*. The sunlit garden where Malvolio is tricked and the dark room where he is imprisoned are other examples where lighting can be used to establish mood. If the production is set in the Elizabethan period, artificial lighting could be used to enhance the use of onstage candles or torches. The play has a number of intimate domestic interiors, so lighting can be used to establish a warm atmosphere.

The play's title implies that it takes place just after Christmas so the weather is likely to be cold. A director may choose to transpose the play to a new location. For example, Stephen Beresford's 2004 production was set in India where lighting evoked the intense heat.

*Twelfth Night* by the RSC.

## Exam tip

Although some directors may choose to change or adapt some aspects of a play, it is important in your exam to show you are aware of:

- stage directions
- information given about the play.

You should include this in your responses.

## Sound

Sound can be important in establishing location, suggesting mood or creating the historical period. A production of the play set in the 1920s began with a piano playing music from the period. Another reordered the first scenes, opening with a terrific storm and shipwreck. The atmosphere of Olivia's garden might be enhanced with birdsong. Music is very important in *Twelfth Night*, as it can be used to reflect the anguish of Orsino's love, the raucous partying of Sir Toby and his friends and the festive singing of Feste. Music is a theme running through the play from 'if music be the food of love' in the opening scene to Feste's soulful 'the rain it raineth every day' – suggesting that troubles never end – at its close.

## Activity ?

### Lighting design

Examine the text for details of implied lighting. Shakespeare did not indicate lighting effects, as there was no stage lighting in his theatre. There are, however, lines of dialogue that tell the audience about the weather and time of day. For example, in **Act 2, Scene 3** the drunken group enter talking of 'being up after midnight', thus communicating that the scene takes place late at night. Decide how you would use stage lighting to create appropriate moods and atmosphere for each scene the play.

Costume design.

## Glossary

**Hierarchical**: Arranged in order of rank.

**Nuance**: A subtle shade of meaning.

**Nihilistic**: The rejection of all religious and moral principles, often in the belief that life is meaningless.

## DNA by Dennis Kelly

### Performance and social context

*DNA* by Dennis Kelly was written in 2007 for the National Theatre Connections project, which pairs young actors with new writing. It was performed by over 40 youth groups across the UK. The playwright stipulated that the names and genders could be changed to suit the groups performing the play, so John could become Jane and Leah could become Lee. *DNA* was also performed by a cast of young professional actors at the National Theatre in a programme designed to encourage young people to go to the theatre. It was presented on a bare stage with back projection creating the different locations. *DNA* is a dark, chilling and **nihilistic** play, examining teenage gang culture and their **hierarchical** power structures, and the nature of guilt and responsibility. The play captures the **nuances** of teenage conversation with overlapping dialogue and incomplete sentences punctuated by outbursts of emotion. It is both a shocking examination of cruelty and at times a black comedy. *DNA* questions whether the group is more important than the individual against a background of mercilessness, moving between everyday and horrifying events. The social background to the play is 21st-century Britain where teenagers are frequently portrayed in the media as lawless and without morality. They are often shown as being without parental control, plaguing citizens in shopping centres and disrupting schools. The newspapers show stereotypical images of a young person wearing a 'hoodie' with a blank expression or as part of a dangerous looking group lurking on a street. TV images of young people among the looters in the London riots (August 2011) would seem to justify this opinion. However, Dennis Kelly did not intend the teenagers in *DNA* to fit any perceived norm. In *DNA* the gang find unity in the aftermath of their crime and no character leaves unchanged.

### The story of *DNA*

The title **DNA** refers to the use of the genetic material found at the scene of a crime or on a piece of evidence that can be tested for links to a suspect. The play is divided into four acts, marked one to four in the text, with each act having a number of scenes. The playwright suggests that the names and genders of the characters are only suggestions and can be changed to suit any cast: they are more symbolic of personality types than fully rounded individuals.

### Act 1

The action begins with Jan and Mark in a street discussing a mysterious death. Later it is revealed that the dead boy is Adam, a bullied victim of the gang. We find out that after cruelly taunting and hurting Adam, gang members lured him onto a grille covering a deep shaft, made him walk across it while they threw stones at him and finally he fell into the hole, presumed dead. They try to justify their vicious attack on him by saying he was laughing. Phil, a largely silent but menacing character, devises a carefully orchestrated cover-up to frame a non-existent person.

Phil and Richard.

Three of the gang are told to break into Adam's house and steal a jumper and shoes then, without touching the jumper, place it in a new plastic bin liner, thus avoiding DNA contamination. Brian and Richard, weak followers of the gang, are to tell the headmaster that Brian has been 'flashed' by a 'fat postman with bad teeth' in the woods. Lou, Danny and Jan are instructed to lay a trail of footprints in the woods, while Cathy and Mark are to drop Adam's jumper in the street when there is a passing male stranger: he will pick it up and run after them 'covering it in DNA'. The final instruction is that the man must be asked to put the jumper straight into the 'charity shop' bin liner.

## Act 2

Adam is reported missing. The police have found a man that fits the description of the man that Phil concocted because Cathy used her 'initiative' to find a man that matched the description. The plan has gone wrong and an innocent man has been accidentally framed. Brian is refusing to go into the police station to identify him but Phil threatens him with being taken 'up to the grille' if he doesn't go. Brian complies and identifies this innocent man.

## Act 3

Cathy discovers Adam, alive and living in the woods: he has clearly lost his mind. In a shocking twist, Phil takes charge. He demonstrates to Cathy how to kill Adam with a plastic bag.

## Act 4

The play ends with Phil and Richard in a field after the circumstances of that death have been revealed and the characters' lives have changed forever.

---

### Activity ?

**Reconstruct Phil's plan**

Read from page 23, John Tate: 'So. What do we do?' to page 26, Phil: 'Any questions?'

1   In a group, one student should play Phil, while Cathy, Danny, Mark, Richard, Brian, the headmaster, Lou, Jan and the man who picks up the jumper are **multi-roled** by everyone else. Phil acts as the **narrator** for the events – he should speak the text or improvise the instructions.

2   Include a variety of drama techniques, for example, using **slow motion** or speaking **thoughts aloud**.

3   If possible, film the final version and watch it. Discuss what this scene reveals about Phil's power. Who is to blame for the consequences?

### Glossary

**Multi-role**: When one actor plays more than character in a play.

## Character

The director's ideas for the play will determine how the actors approach their roles. How the characters are portrayed will differ from one production to another. Every character is responsible for Adam's death and the cover-up in some way.

The key characters and some words that can describe them:

| Phil | Menacing  Cold  Sinister |
|---|---|
| John Tate | Controlling  Manipulative  Tyrannical |
| Leah | Insecure  Loyal  Insightful |
| Mark | Cruel  Malicious  Ruthless |
| Jan | Bullying Intimidating Gullible |
| Danny | Ambitious  Fearful  Sceptical |
| Richard | Insecure  Confident  Sycophant |
| Cathy | Volatile  Sadistic  Merciless |
| Brian | Nervous  Introverted  Vulnerable |
| Lou | Unsuspecting Impressionable  Spineless |

## Activity ?

On a large sheet of paper, or on a computer, create a mind map for all the characters. Find quotations from the play to support your thinking. The example below shows a mind map for Danny. You do not have to use the words from the chart – decide for yourself how you see each of the teenagers.

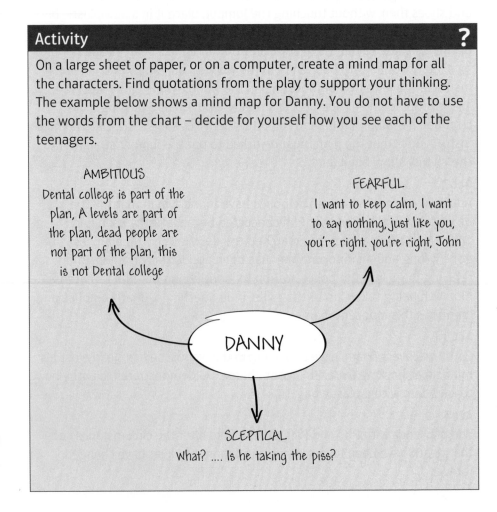

AMBITIOUS
Dental college is part of the plan, A levels are part of the plan, dead people are not part of the plan, this is not Dental college

FEARFUL
I want to keep calm, I want to say nothing, just like you, you're right. you're right, John

DANNY

SCEPTICAL
What? .... Is he taking the piss?

## Creating impact

The play explores the dynamics of a group or gang and the struggle for power or status. At its heart lies the debate about why humans commit unspeakable crimes. The children who abducted, tortured and murdered the toddler James Bulger in 1993 were 10 years old. They appeared to be victims of painful circumstances, but could they have been born evil? *DNA*'s power lies in Kelly's retelling of the horrific events through reported dialogue: there are very few scenes of violence on stage. The impact on the audience comes from the verbal recreation of abuse and torture and from the reporting of the consequences of Phil's plan for concealment. In approaching the text, the cast and the director will determine the intended impact on the audience.

## Performing characters in *DNA*

In your exam you will be asked to interpret an extract from the play. Some questions will concern your approach to playing a character, some will ask you to think from the point of view of a designer and some will require you to comment on how a director would work with an actor to realise a performance. Kelly's dialogue captures the realism of everyday conversation: half-finished sentences overlap with interruptions. Many of the speeches are short and sentences incomplete. In contrast are the monologues from Leah and later from Richard.

Leah, whose admiration and love for Phil makes her blind to his manipulative power, appears to be the most insightful and knowledgeable of the gang. She has views on man's evolution from the apes, global warming, 'the beauty and fragility of reality' and of her happiness at seeing a sunset. She talks endlessly to herself, ignored by Phil, but her ramblings include moments of pathos, shock and humour. Her long monologues provide both a challenge and an opportunity for an actor.

---

### Activity ?

**Working on a monologue**

Read Leah's monologue in Act 2, Scene 2 'Are you happy' to 'What have we done Phil?'

1. Divide the speech into sections, then label each section. For example, labels could include:  What makes us happy? or Killing my pet. [If possible, work on a photocopy: make notes and use highlighters to indicate your ideas.]

2. How do you want to affect the **audience**? Indicate significant lines or sections of the text.

3. Think about how to use **pause** to create meaning and tension.

4. How might you vary your **voice** to convey Leah's emotion? Do you think Leah would **move** during this speech? If so, indicate where and why: if not, how would her **stillness** create impact?

---

### Activity ?

**Acts of cruelty**

Read Act 3, Scene 3 (p. 49) where Adam appears from 'They stand around a boy who looks like a tramp' to 'I'm not coming back. *Beat*. It's Adam'.

1. How might you use the stage space to reflect the atmosphere at this point in the play?

2. Consider how voices can heighten the mood. Think about **tone**, **emphasis** and **inflection**.

3. How can you create the atmosphere of menace with the use of **pause**, **facial expression or eye contact**?

4. There are few stage directions so you will need to think about the use of **physical skills** and **stage space**.

5. Rehearse this scene and show it to others in your group.

---

### Exam tip

Examiners will expect your answers to show the intended **impact** on the audience and state the way your interpretation creates **meaning**. However, these exact words may not appear in the question.

## Working on the text as a director of *DNA*

Throughout the play there are power struggles between the gang members. Phil and John Tate have the most authority while Leah, through her insecurity and desire to be loved, has little influence. Danny, Jan and Mark follow the lead of Phil and are in awe of John's menacing control. In the group scenes there is a battle for status within the followers, as well as the leaders. An actor playing any role in *DNA* will need to consider how his character's relationship with others in the scenes is communicated in performance.

*DNA* has been described as short, sharp and shocking. The impact the production has on an audience will be a result of both the power of the acting performances and the choices made by the director.

### Activity ?

**Playing your character's status**

Read Act 1, Scene 3 from '*Lou*: 'He's dead, John' to 'I think we should tell someone' then use director Max Stafford-Clarke's playing cards technique from page 7 in the Page to stage section of this book.

1  Remove jokers and picture cards from a pack and take one card each. Do not show it to anyone.

2  This card is your status – 10 the highest and an ace the lowest. The colour/suit is not important.

3  Play the first part of this extract up to 'No one say that word, okay, no one'. Behave according to the status indicated by the card – for example, John might have picked out a 2. Now discuss how this influenced your use of voice, movement and **proxemics**.

4  What card you would give each character in this extract? John Tate is probably a 10 – play the scene again. What is different? How did this new card value influence your performance choices?

### Glossary

**Proxemics**: The relationship and position between actors in the performance space or the position of actors in relation to the audience.

### Activity ?

**Creating an impact on an audience**

Read Act 1, Scene 2 where Jan and Mark describe the sequence of events leading to Adam's fall through the grille, from 'So, you want us to tell them' to 'So. What do we do?'

1  As a director, note words to describe the desired audience response, e.g. tearful or shocked.

2  Make notes on the extract showing how you would direct the actors in order to produce this reaction. Give examples of performance skills, e.g. facial expression, vocal tone, movement, rather than directions about where to move on the stage.

3  Work in a group to try out your different directing ideas.

## Designing for a production of *DNA*

*DNA* is set in an indeterminate place and time in a space suggestive of three recurring locations. These settings are all outside and public – a street, a field, a wood. The designer must suggest, rather than realistically create, these places. Sound, lighting and costume combine to convey location, mood and atmosphere. The design for the first production at the National Theatre in 2008 staged the play on a bare stage with back projection.

Set design at the National Theatre, 2008.

Box set design for Hull Truck, 2012.

The 2012 production by Hull Truck, designed and directed by Anthony Banks, added a strip of artificial turf laid over a floor-cloth, which was symbolically marked out with DNA QR codes. The ease of flow from one scene to another is important, as any break in the action would detract from the emotional power of the play. The actors can create variations in levels physically, removing the need to have rostra or any stage furniture.

## Costume

*DNA* demands contemporary clothing that reflects the reality in which these young people live. Costume can reveal personality through style choices made by individuals but in *DNA* the conformity of the gang culture also has an influence. The colours the designer selects might suggest character traits, for example, red could show confidence while implying danger. However, designers would be unlikely to costume a jealous character in green because that's just too obvious! Leah's costume may show that she does not want to draw attention to herself with loud clothing and Danny's costume might infer that he is from a middle-class family who aspire for him to become a dentist. Consideration of style, texture, colour and shape will reveal the individual characteristics of each person, while maintaining the cohesion of the gang. Adam's injuries could be created with stage make-up, using liquid latex for the scars, and stage blood.

A costume designer would draw designs for every character and mount them side by side so that they could be viewed in relation to each other.

### Activity ?

**Think as a designer**

1. Collect pictures of the three locations in *DNA* from newspapers, magazines or online.

2. Make a collage with three sections – the street, a field, the woods.

3. Note the atmosphere. Where does the light come from? What is the mood?

4. Which images do you think match your own ideas for the settings in *DNA*? How could you suggest them on stage?

# Section A Bringing texts to life

## Activity ?

### Designing *DNA*

1   In a group of four, choose two characters each. Look at contemporary fashions online or in magazines and decide on clothing styles and colours for each character.

2   Working alone on your two characters, collect images of as many different ideas as possible. Cut them out or print them and stick them onto a sheet of paper – one for each character.

3   Now use these ideas to come up with your own design. Draw and colour your costume on a blank piece of A4 paper and label it to show colour, texture, material and style.

4   Share the designs with your group and place the sketches side by side. Discuss the different effects.

## Exam tip

Remember to look carefully at the printed extract for evidence. Information will be found in stage directions and dialogue.

## Props

Personal properties can communicate age and personality traits. There is no stage furniture specified in the *DNA* script but props are suggested throughout the text. The most significant props are used by Phil, who is frequently eating or drinking: an ice cream, a can of coke, a bag of crisps, sweets and muffins, which he keeps in his carrier bag. The playwright indicates where Phil eats or puts down his drink. The actor uses these props to punctuate the dialogue or to create tension. Leah has a plastic tub and later a suitcase and there is also the chilling plastic bag that will be used to kill Adam. Other personal props could be included – mobile phones, handbags, make-up.

## Lighting

Lighting can suggest mood, atmosphere, and time of day or location. A combination of lighting and back projection enables the designer to create varied settings. Clues from the text can inform decisions.

For example, at the end of Act 2, Leah says 'Look at that sky. Have you ever seen a sky like that?' The director and designers would discuss their interpretation of 'that sky' then the designers would create an effect using lighting and back projection to fit with their ideas.

The source of light is also important. Afternoon summer sunshine comes from overhead, whereas in a street at dusk the light will be low and fading. The light in a wood will be filtered through tree branches and different shadows will be cast according to the time of day. The action of *DNA* takes place over a few weeks, so the season would not change. The first time we see Phil, he is eating an ice cream – perhaps it is summer? In the woods in Act 3, the atmosphere is of threat and danger. The season is unchanged, so possibly it is a drizzly evening with shadowy corners and a grey, cloudy sky.

## Sound

Sound is very important in a production of *DNA*. Sound conjures the imagined places, helping to make them real for the audience. Traffic noise, car horns or police sirens suggest a busy city street; birdsong reflects the atmosphere of a wood. The sound designer will consider the intended mood of the scene, for example, if dark events are unfolding in the wood, birdsong might not be appropriate as we associate it with tranquillity. The occasional squawk of a crow could evoke the threatening mood. Music was not written in by the playwright but will be important in linking the scenes, adding to the pace and emotion, as well as providing a contemporary setting.

## *1984* adapted from the novel by George Orwell by Robert Icke and Duncan Macmillan

### Historical context

George Orwell's 1949 novel *1984* is a culturally significant yet complex text featuring a character called Winston Smith. It is a story rooted in popular culture by the television shows **Big Brother** and **Room 101**. This play version is the result of a collaboration between Headlong, a theatre company renowned for its groundbreaking re-imaginings of classic plays, and the Almeida Theatre, London in 2013. The adaptation takes the little-read appendix of the book as its framework. This is called the Appendix: The Principles of Newspeak, it is mentioned in a footnote on page 3 of the novel but few readers ever look at it after finishing the book. Newspeak refers to the invented language that is being implemented in the novel. By structuring the play in this way, the playwrights force the modern audience to ask questions about what they are watching. Is Winston Smith's account of **the Party** (the political party in control) the work of an unpredictable narrator? Or is it a record of life in 1984 before the downfall of the Party? The playwrights provoke the modern audience into questioning who should take responsibility for the erosion (wearing away) of individual liberty. Could it be them?

### Performance context

*1984* was first performed by Headlong Theatre at Nottingham Playhouse in September 2013. The set design was dominated by a huge screen where words and images were projected. The stage was a proscenium arch with the audience in tiered seating. The writers wanted to adapt the novel in a way that made it accessible to a young audience whilst also engaging people who knew the book very well.

**What does *1984* mean to a modern audience? Orwell wrote *1984* as World War II ended and Britain was a single state. Today we are joined with Europe in the 'Eurozone' and bound by a treaty to join allies in distant wars. Winston Smith is an 'everyman' figure with whom the audience identifies, seeing events played over and over again through his eyes. Themes of psychological pressure, personal freedom and eyes everywhere run throughout the play. These ask the 21st-century audience to question society: a society obsessed with screens. We stare at screens in shops, on laptops, tablets and phones. We live in a world of 24/7 communication and constant rolling news updates allowing us to watch global events unfolding. But the information age also impacts our privacy: Wikileaks can spread classified information across the globe at the touch of a button, phone tapping invades privacy of victims and celebrities, while CCTV cameras 'keep us safe'. Orwell describes 'Newspeak'; we reduce our language to 140 characters on Twitter and telescope words for advertising and convenience: 'ringtone', 'jetwash', 'travelogue'. The play's fictional events are unsettlingly mirrored on our own screens: in the 'Two Minutes Hate' a Thoughtcriminal appears with a bag over his head to make a televised 'confession' before being shot in the head, chillingly reminiscent of ISIS videos.**

### Taking it further

To listen to a voice recording of an interview with the playwrights Robert Icke and Duncan Macmillan talking about *1984*, go to the Theatre Voice website and search for 'Robert Icke'.

### The story of *1984*

The play opens with a clock striking 13 and an unseen voice introducing Winston Smith, who begins to write a diary. The scene moves to a dusty reading room where people are discussing a novel. Is this a post 2050 'book group' or members of the Party examining a revolutionary text from the past? Winston remains visible and someone suggests that they are 'inside his head'. The play frequently jumps about in time and location. The narrative unfolds in a disjointed and reflective style: both looking at the past and dreaming of a better future. The play quite deliberately leaves the audience wondering, along with Winston, do you know where you are?

Winston is sceptical about the Party and doubts the existence of **Big Brother**. He works at the soulless **Ministry of Truth** with Syme, where his job is to delete those who have committed thoughtcrime from the records. He meets Julia, who shares his revolutionary ideas, and they fall quickly in love and meet secretly in an antique shop. This is a 'sexcrime', forbidden by the Party. Eventually, Winston and Julia confess to O'Brien, whom they believe to be a member of the **Brotherhood**. O'Brien welcomes them, tricks them into making incriminating comments and arranges for Winston to be given a copy of 'the book', a volume written by their leader, Emmanuel Goldstein. Julia and Winston are caught. Winston is taken to the **Ministry of Love**, where O'Brien, who had been watching him, tortures him in order to change his way of thinking. Winston must believe in **doublethink**: he knows 2+2 = 4 but is forced to admit that it could be 5. Finally, he is taken to the dreaded Room 101 where he faces his worst fear – rats. Despite promising never to betray Julia he finally cries: 'Do it to Julia!' The play ends with Winston drinking coffee in a café where he meets an older and much changed Julia. The scene then returns to the reading room discussion.

### Vocabulary of *1984*

**Room 101**: The Ministry of Love's torture chamber.

**The Party**: The one-party state with no elected government.

**Big Brother**: The perceived leader of the Party.

**The Brotherhood**: A secret revolutionary group plotting to overthrow Big Brother and the Party.

**Newspeak**: A language, developed by the Party, to reduce the number of words.

**Ministry of Truth**: A building devoted to creating propaganda.

**Ministry of Love**: Detention centre for political dissidents.

**Thoughtcrime**: Expressing negative thoughts about the Party or Big Brother.

**Doublethink**: To hold two contradictory opinions at the same time and to believe them both.

## Characters

The characters in *1984* are a combination of believable individuals and symbols of their wider meaning. For example, while the audience can understand Winston and Julia as people, Winston also represents the 'everyman'. Syme and O'Brien are symbols of the repressive and repressed in this dystopian world. Some characters are reminders that this play is switching in time, for example, The Mother, whereas the Thoughtcriminal and Goldstein appear only on the screen.

Key characters and some words that can describe them:

| | |
|---|---|
| Winston Smith | Sensitive  Mild  Defiant |
| O'Brien | Terrifying  Duplicitous  Ruthless |
| Syme | Sly  Sarcastic  Accepting |
| Julia | Rebellious    Complex    Resilient |
| Parsons | Obedient  Unquestioning  Naive |
| Charrington | Generous  Calm  Deceptive |

## Creating impact

A production of *1984* should have an intense impact. The visual and sound effects remind the modern audience of the horrors of Orwell's imagined future, while the characters and structure caution against complacency. Impact is created through the decisions of actors and directors in addition to the technical elements.

---

**Activity**  **?**

Watch the Headlong Trailer for *1984*, by going to YouTube and searching for 'Trailer: Headlong Theatre's 1984'. How does this trailer make you feel? How does it make an impact on your senses? What would you expect to see in this production?

---

**Activity**  **?**

### Room 101

Winston is taken to the infamous Room 101 in the later stages of the play. His torture with his worst fear, rats, is one of the most disturbing and powerful scenes.

1  Read from page 85 *An animal handler wheels a trolley …* to *the sound of the rats is overwhelming.*

2  In a group of three, discuss your ideas for staging this scene to create an impact on the audience. How do you want them to feel?

3  If possible, create the sound effects digitally and use the lighting in your drama space. Put your ideas into practice with one of the group operating the sound and light and the others becoming Winston and O'Brien.

4  Try the scene in different ways, exploring how the production elements and the performances are combined to make an impact on the audience.

# Section A Bringing texts to life

## Activity ?

### Explaining Newspeak

In pairs, read pages 26–7 'You don't really appreciate Newspeak, Winston' to 'Orthodoxy is unconsciousness'. Read the speech aloud, alternating after each paragraph.

1   Discuss how you might speak this monologue to enable the audience to understand the principle of Newspeak and the removal of the language of thought.

2   Think about the use of pause, eye contact and variation in tone. Syme asks Winston questions but does not expect an answer. How does this change his use of voice?

3   Do you think that Syme would move during this speech? How might he use gesture?

4   Now take it in turns to perform and to direct the speech.

5   Look at the sample exam question. Use your practical work to plan an answer together.

## Working on the text as an actor in *1984*

In the exam, you will be asked to interpret an extract from the play. Some questions will concern your approach to playing a character, some will ask you to think from the point of view of a designer and some will require you to comment on how a director would work with an actor to realise a performance. Macmillan and Icke created this play by taking the text of Orwell's original novel as dialogue. There are important aspects of the world of the play that have to be communicated to an audience. One example is Syme's explanation of Newspeak.

## Exam-style question

You are going to play Syme in this extract. As a performer, give three suggestions of how you would use performance skills to communicate the purpose of Newspeak to an audience. **(6 marks)**

## Working on the text as a director of *1984*

The exam questions will ask you to look at the extract from the viewpoint of a director. You will need to include the decisions made about the overall concept, an actor's performance and the director's ideas for design. In *1984* the audience is taken on a journey through the world of Winston Smith in a totalitarian future world. The challenge for a director is to build belief in the onstage world, while the text constantly asks them to question 'the true reality of things'. The scene where Winston and Julia visit O'Brien, thinking that he is a dissenter, has an almost ceremonial atmosphere. O'Brien's dialogue is almost Biblical in tone, similar to a **catechism** (a summary of the principles of Christian religion in the form of questions and answers, used for religious instruction). O'Brien is trapping Winston and Julia, as their responses are played back to them (and the audience) after O'Brien betrays them.

## Activity ?

### Rehearsing the scene

Read pages 56–7 from 'In general terms, what are you prepared to do?' to [Winston] 'No'.

1   How would you direct the actor playing O'Brien in asking these questions? How might he use pace, voice, pause, movement and eye contact? What impact do you want to have on the audience?

2   Winston and Julia say only 'Yes' or 'No'. How would you work with the actors in exploring each of these answers? Consider vocal tone, volume, emphasis, pause and pace.

3   If possible, record the finished scene and play it back on a screen to recreate the scene later in the play (page 79) when we see the recording of this incriminating evidence.

## Designing for a production of *1984*

The play has been described as 'not merely a visual experience, rather a complete assault on the senses' with visual images, lighting and sound combining to create a powerful effect.

The screen, hung over the stage, is central to the impact of the design. Offstage events, such as Winston and Julia's secret room in the antique shop, are revealed in addition to events broadcast on the telescreens. The play is set in an anonymous, wood-panelled room with a frosted glass window which, when lit, reveals a corridor and side rooms. The back projections create mood, heighten tension and constantly remind the audience of the ever-present telescreens. The era is deliberately ambiguous: is this 1984 or 2050? Or maybe the play is inside Winston's head as he recalls events? Properties and stage furniture communicate locations, including office chairs, canteen trays, desks and office lamps, chocolate and a toolbox. There are key moments when props have a powerful and chilling impact on the audience, for example the torturers' instruments, the thick gloves and protective masks of the animal handlers in Room 101.

*1984* set design.

| Activity | ? |
|---|---|

**What's on the screen?**

1. Examine the play and make a list of everything that is projected on to the screen.

2. What is the impact of each projection? Write notes on the effect on an audience. For example, page 32 states *a montage of images*. The audience identifies with these life events and considers how the Party can erase someone from existence.

## Lighting

Lighting can be used to create mood, increase tension and indicate location in a production. The constant shifting of place and time in *1984*, together with the building of moments of suspense and horror requires intricate lighting design. Throughout the text the playwrights suggest lighting and it is the task of the designer to create appropriate moods and atmosphere and to consider the desired impact on an audience.

A glance at the opening of the play indicates many lighting changes: *a pinspot on Winston's face, a dull red spot* – indicating his nose bleed – *lamps flicking on and off*. Lighting informs the audience of location and mood, for example, the opaque windows in the panelled room are backlit to reveal the corridor, the sun rises and deepens in colour, and blackouts signify a new time or scene. The lighting's most significant function is to disorientate, both the characters within the play and the audience. The 'place where there is no darkness' that O'Brien speaks of is created with lighting that is 'bright, uncomfortable, unforgiving' and when Winston is tortured there is 'a sudden bright light on Winston. The house lights slowly rise' exposing the audience and making them complicit in his suffering.

## Sound

Sound is of utmost importance in this play. When the telescreen is switched off by O'Brien (page 55) there is 'the first real silence in the play': the 'assault on the senses' is relentless. Sound directions are aggressively used to create the world of *1984*. Scripted sounds include sirens screech, gunshots fire, helicopters whirr overhead, bombs drop and a klaxon pierces the ears. Horrific loud screams, disorientating crashes and echoing amplified voices oppress the audience. Sound also locates the action, creates tension and highlights meaning. For example, the shrill child's whistle alerts the Thought Police, which is an uncomfortable reminder of the power the Party has over the young. While the pure simplicity of the nursery rhyme 'Oranges and Lemons' references a past when singing was a sign of happiness, the nursery rhyme morphs into a mobile ringtone in the opening scene, signifying a modern setting.

Photo from the 2013 Headlong production of *1984*, showing HATE on a screen.

## Activity     ?

**Two minutes Hate**

On pages 33–5, read from 'Attention comrades' to 'Two minutes Hate is over, comrades'.

Here are the scripted sounds: *countdown / silence / screaming grinding metallic noise / crowd roaring and screaming / amplified voice / gunshot / cheers / chanting / klaxon.*

The <u>underlined</u> sounds are created by the actors, but could be enhanced by recorded sound.

How important is sound in this scene? Why? What is the intended impact on the audience? Discuss these questions in a group.

Now read the question on the left and plan an answer. There are 14 marks for this answer. You can work on this as a group, in pairs or on your own.

## Exam-style question

Discuss how you would use sound to enhance the production of this extract for the audience.

**(14 marks)**

## Costume

Icke and Macmillan are very clear in their notes that they wanted the design to capture the concept that the play is a series of flashbacks to things that have already happened rather than to set it in a specific time or place. 'I think it is profoundly dishonest to do the blue overalls April the 4th version of *1984*'. The play opens with a group studying a book in a 'wood panelled room' with characters in costumes that evoke the 1940s, when the novel was written. There is no suggestion of the blue overalls or 'futuristic' costumes mentioned in the novel. Costume shows status – Winston and Syme work in an office but O'Brien has a high position in the Party. The Thoughtcriminal and Goldstein, who appear on the telescreen, are costumed to show their status and their fate. The Torturers' and the Animal Handlers' costumes add to the horror of the scenes.

## Exam tip

Your answer should show an understanding of the complete play; therefore, references to the importance of sound overall would be expected.

## Taking it further

Icke and Macmillan made a deliberate decision that *1984* wouldn't be a straight reproduction of George Orwell's novel. Find out more about the freedom and liberties that they took when adapting the book into their play by searching for 'Headlong's adaptation of 1984' and reading the transcript of the discussion between director and playwright.

## Blue Stockings by Jessica Swale

### Historical context

*Blue Stockings,* first performed at The Globe Theatre in London in 2013, charts the struggle of female students fighting for academic equality at Cambridge University. The play is set in 1896 at Girton College. Situated just outside of the centre of Cambridge, the college was established in 1869 as a place for women to study. By 1898 it was home to female undergraduates, staff, and some male colleagues sympathetic to the cause of female academia. Students today may regard attitudes to women at that time as extremely old-fashioned. Women were allowed to attend lectures, but the university refused to award them degrees. Women at Girton were subjected to appalling hostility from male undergraduates who patronised or bullied them. They were chaperoned when they attended mixed lectures and were not allowed to meet male students unsupervised. The play opens with a speech by Dr Henry Maudsley, the renowned psychiatrist, who refers to academic women as 'blue stockings' and warns that giving women degrees is 'a dangerous idea'. In 1898, when the Senate of the university debated this issue, an effigy of a 'blue stocking' on a bicycle was burnt on the streets of Cambridge. In the background of the play are the suffragists who were fighting their own battle for women to be allowed to vote.

Girton College Cambridge circa 1898.

### Performance and contemporary context

The first production of *Blue Stockings* was at The Globe Theatre in London. The Globe is a reconstruction of Shakespeare's theatre and was built as an exact replica of the original building. In recent years directors of The Globe have staged modern as well as Elizabethan plays. *Blue Stockings* was performed on a thrust stage with some of the audience seated in the surrounding balconies and others standing where the groundlings had stood to watch Shakespeare's plays. At the back of the stage the set designer created the turrets of Girton College and the various locations were suggested with props and stage furniture that could be moved on and off the stage very quickly: for example, chairs, tables, bookshelves and bicycles. The costumes indicated the era with the male students in white shirts with black waistcoats or jackets and the female students in white shirts with white pantaloons and black boots or coloured ankle-length day dresses.

The text of *Blue Stockings* is dedicated to Malala Yousafzai, a Pakistani activist for female education. Malala's father ran a school in Pakistan: he was an outspoken critic of the Taliban, who banned girls from going to school. In 2012, aged 15, Malala was shot in the head for defying the ban. She survived the initial attack and was flown to Birmingham in a critical condition, where she received life-saving surgery. There was international outrage following this attack. In 2014 Malala was awarded the Nobel Peace Prize for her campaign for female education.

Many challenges face women all around the world who are attempting to gain an education and they are often subjected to sexism and violence. Other examples of sexist attitudes in our society include the abuse received on Twitter by Mary Beard, professor of classics at Cambridge University, when she campaigned for the female novelist, Jane Austen, to appear on a £10 banknote.

## The story of *Blue Stockings*

### Act 1

The play opens with the arrival of the new students at Cambridge in September 1896. The male students are welcomed by the famous psychiatrist Dr Henry Maudsley, who lectures them on scientific findings which demonstrate that women who exercise their brains will lose the ability to bear children. Dr Elizabeth Welsh, who speaks about the idea of degrees for women, welcomes the new female students. Four female students introduce themselves as they wait for the eccentric Mr Banks, who teaches them about Newton's second law by making them ride a bicycle. In their first lectures the female students are told about Mrs Welsh's campaign for women to be awarded degrees. In a mixed lecture with Dr Maudsley female students are ignored and Tess Moffat is humiliated, then ejected, when she challenges his claims. Will Bennett, a friend of Tess from home and a secret admirer, is excluded by his friends for knowing a 'Girtonite'. Studying in the library, Tess flirts surreptitiously with Ralph Mayhew, meets him secretly and falls in love. Her determination to achieve at the highest level appears to weaken.

As this relationship develops Tess is warned by both the other female students and by her friend Will that Ralph may not be as honourable as he appears. Maeve Sullivan receives bad news when her brother, Billy, arrives in Cambridge: her mother has died, leaving Maeve's young siblings in need of care. Billy insists that she leaves the university and returns home. Despite Maeve's fervent argument that she should be able to complete her education, Mrs Welsh decides that Maeve's responsibility lies with her family. In his lecture to the men at Trinity, Mr Banks distributes a first-class student essay: they are shocked to learn that it was written by a first year from Girton – Tess.

### Taking it further

Find out more about Malala Yousafzai. There is a BBC documentary about her as well as the film *He named me Malala*.

Tess and Will study the stars (Act 2, Scene 3).

# Section A Bringing texts to life

### Activity

1  Read Act 1, Scene 8 from 'Look about what happened in the street…' to '…just give up'

2  Imagine that you are playing Will in this section – answer the following questions: 'How sorry am I out of 10 when I visit Tess?' (10 is extremely sorry and 1 is not sorry at all) 'What outcome do I want?' For example, 'I am sorry 9 out of 10 and I want her to forgive me because I really love her'.

3  Look in detail at the scene. How would you use performance skills to convey your emotions to an audience?

4  You can extend this exercise by working with a partner who plays Tess. Her questions are 'How angry am I about Will's behaviour in the street?', 'What do I want to happen when he visits my room?'

5  Now play the section and discuss how the answers to your questions affected your use of performance skills.

## Act 2

The campaign for women to be awarded degrees gathers force and its supporters are pushed to make stark choices: Mr Banks gives up a prestigious promotion so that he can continue to lecture at Girton, but is later sacked. Miss Blake chooses to resign rather than compromise her beliefs. Excitement builds when the vote is granted and the women buy material for banners. Lloyd visits the shop and makes an inflammatory speech belittling all female students: the outraged owner, Mrs Lindley, throws him out. Tess is heartbroken when Will tells her that Ralph is to be engaged to a student from the less radical Newnham College. The following morning Tess, whose written papers are outstanding, does badly in her **viva**. A pass requires 'excellence across the board', so she fails. Mrs Welsh, however, offers her the opportunity to return the following year to resit the exam and continue her studies. Voting day arrives, trainloads of men who oppose women's rights have arrived in Cambridge and there are ugly scenes on the streets. The vote is lost but the play ends triumphantly on the Cambridge railway station platform where Will and Tess declare their love for one another.

### Character

The director's ideas for the play will not only determine how the actors approach their roles but also how the characters portrayed will differ from one production to another.

Key characters and some words that can describe them:

| Tess Moffat (Girton student) | Self-assured  Curious  Assertive |
|---|---|
| Celia Willbond (Girton student) | Diligent  Delicate  Nervous |
| Carolyn Addison (Girton student) | Confident  Outgoing  Privileged |
| Maeve Sullivan (Girton Student) | Tough  Determined  Honest |
| Elizabeth Welsh (mistress of Girton College) | Passionate  Shrewd  Patient |
| Mr Banks (lecturer at Girton and Trinity) | Calm  Principled  Eccentric |
| Miss Blake (lecturer at Girton) | Uncompromising  Loyal  Enthusiastic |
| Ralph Mayhew (student at Trinity) | Cruel  Egotistic  Arrogant |
| Will Bennett (student at Trinity) | Kind-hearted  Honourable  Reliable |

You will be asked to write about how you would play a character from your performance text. The section from Scene 8 outlined in the activity is of a similar length to the one that will be printed on your exam paper. Below is an example exam question for this section.

### Exam-style question

You are going to play Will. He is probably the most honourable male student in the play. Give **three** suggestions of how you would use performance skills to show this in the extract. **(6 marks)**

## Exam tip

Always look at the number of marks given for each answer. In the example there are **6 marks** available. There are three suggested marks for an answer with a reason for each idea.

For example, your answer might talk about performance skills and the reasons for using them. These have been marked in the example below using PS and R.

**PS** Moving awkwardly from one foot to the other, avoiding eye contact, when he begins to explain his behaviour in the street. **R** This shows that he feels guilty about what happened and he knows that it was wrong.

**PS** An urgent, yet gentle, tone of voice when he tells Tess that he has promised her father that he will look after her. **R** To show that he cares about Tess and wants to convince her not to put her reputation in jeopardy.

**PS** Moving close to Tess, holding her lightly by the shoulders and looking into her eyes when he says, in a soft, quiet voice, 'there are plenty of fellows who'd give their right arm for you'. **R** To communicate to the audience that he is in love with Tess and to show that he is willing to risk being excluded by his friends.

## Creating impact in a performance of *Blue Stockings*

The central idea of the play is to examine Victorian attitudes to women's education. Several scenes in the play appear outrageous to a modern audience. At The Globe, audiences frequently booed scenes where male students or lecturers humiliated the Girton women. In Act 1, Scene 4, Dr Maudsley humiliates Tess when she questions his 'progressive' theories about female hysteria. The atmosphere in the lecture is volatile: Tess is crushed and mortified both by Dr Maudsley's terse responses to her questions and by the jeering of the male students.

## Exam tip

Examiners will expect your answers to show the intended **impact** on the audience and the way your interpretation creates **meaning**. These exact words may not appear in the question.

## Working as an actor in *Blue Stockings*

In your exam you will be asked to interpret an extract from the play. Some questions will concern your approach to playing a character, some will ask you to think from the point of view of a designer and some will require you to suggest ways in which a director would work with an actor to realise a performance. In Act 2, Scene 6, Carolyn and Tess are buying materials to make banners to support the vote when Lloyd and Edwards come into Mrs Lindley's shop. The men are dismissive of the women's struggle to be allowed to graduate and a heated argument develops. Lloyd explodes in a rage and is thrown out of the haberdashery store by Mrs Lindley.

## Activity ?

Read Act 1, Scene 4 from 'let's abandon the fanciful speculation' to 'I should throw the whole lot of you out'.

1   Work on this section in a group. What impact do you want to have on the audience? Think about gesture and facial expression, vocal tone and volume, movement and stillness.

2   Consider the pace of the scene. Dr Maudsley might be controlled and deliberate and the male students energetic and animated.

3   Actors and directors might action this scene to indicate what effect they want to have. Actions for Dr Maudsley's replies to Tess might include *belittles, humiliates, dismisses, scorns*.

# Section A Bringing texts to life

## Activity  ?

Read Act 2, Scene 6 from 'What would you do with a degree anyway?' to the end of the scene.

Imagine that you are going to play Lloyd in this extract. His function in this scene is to show men's extreme attitudes to women during this era and the playwright does not want the audience to sympathise with his opinions.

At The Globe where the play was first performed, audiences cheered when Mrs Lindley told him to 'Get out'.

Make notes about how you would use performance skills to play Lloyd in the scene.

Read the exam question and look at the example student notes opposite and write (or highlight) your notes in three colours – one for each point that you would make in your answer.

## Exam-style question  ○

You are going to play Lloyd. As a performer, give **three** suggestions of how you would use performance skills to show his attitudes to women's role in society in this extract.

**(6 marks)**

Move towards Tess, getting closer and closer on each phrase right up to her face maintain eye contact– wants to intimidate her. 'Run the country' sneering vocal tone because he dismisses women's ability 'Be an engineer' + 'Develop a cure...'– in an aggressive tone to show he is becoming more angry which leads to the 'explosion' later.

Stress 'man' 'your' and 'you' to emphasise the gender bias.

Explodes – slam hand down on counter and sweep materials to the floor. Move around the space unable to stand still as out of control until 'We are the future' Still – command centre of space, expansive arm gesture to show his total belief that men are more important. Vocal emphasis on each word spoken at the same pace 'We – are – the – future'.

Common whore – moves behind Carolyn, slowly– touches her shoulders in a lustful, disrespectful way because he wants to belittle her and make her feel uncomfortable

Vocal tone to Mrs Lindley contemptuous – he thinks she is just a servant and deserves no respect. Condescending tone 'now if you'd be so kind'. to show his disdain for her, she is just a shopkeeper and has no right to an opinion Look at women on 'Ladies' stockings, to taunt them – point to Tess's legs on Blue Stockings to demean their status in the university

## Working on the text as a director of *Blue Stockings*

The director interprets the text, working with the performers and the designers to create a unique production of the play. The director will have a clear vision of the concept but will work with actors and designers during rehearsals creatively to explore the text. The rowdy drinking game in Scene 8 is the backdrop for the account of Ralph's newfound love. There are only four actors in the scene: it should be noisy and active while communicating to the audience that Ralph has moved on from his relationship with Tess. The men are playing the card game called King of Hearts and drinking brandy. Directors will often explore a scene through improvisation and exercises before looking in detail at the text.

## Activity  ?

1   In a group of four, improvise a scene where a group of friends are playing cards and drinking. During the game you must discuss something unrelated. For example, playing Snap while talking about school dinners. You will realise how difficult it is to keep the game going while talking about something else. Use a real pack of cards if possible.

2   Now try this exercise again with a different game and a different conversation topic. Before starting the improvisation everyone chooses a card: the person with the highest card must decide on something that they want to tell the group and find a way to bring this into the conversation during the card game.

3   Read the scene and decide how you might direct it so that it is fast-paced and boisterous with all the important details communicated to the audience.

## Working as a designer for *Blue Stockings*

The set for this play requires the designer to establish multiple locations. The original production was staged at the The Globe on a bare stage, therefore properties and costumes were equally important in conveying the place, time and atmosphere. The set designer's initial examination of the play would involve listing all the places suggested by the playwright. It would not be possible to change the set every time there is a new scene so the designer will create a set that will suggest the different locations with stage furniture, props and lighting.

### Activity ?

Create a chart similar to the one below, listing all the scenes. Make notes on the locations and times of day for each scene. There are 12 scenes in each Act.

| Act 1 | Location | Time of day | Act 2 | Location | Time of day |
|---|---|---|---|---|---|
| 3 | | | 3 | Hilltop | Evening |
| 4 | Lecture Hall | Morning | 4 | | |
| 8 | Tess's room | Evening | 8 | | |
| 9 | | | 9 | The Orchard | Night |

Now make some sketches or find images of how each location would look.

### Lighting

Lighting can enhance the mood as well as suggesting locations. In *Blue Stockings* the multiple scenes can be conveyed with lighting effects. In Act 1, Scene 1 the lighting might suggest a bright September morning, while in Act 2, Scene 5 lighting that evokes moonlight with deep shadows of trees communicates the orchard at night. The source of light informs the lighting designer's choice of effects. In scenes in lecture halls, drawing rooms and studies the source would be ceiling lights and table lamps. In contrast, outdoor scenes would be lit naturally by the sun or moon, the intensity of this light would be determined by cloud cover and season. The scene where Tess and Ralph discuss the stars is a clear night where the stars are visible, whereas in Act 1, Scene 9 the orchard is dark and Tess cannot see Ralph until he startles her. Lighting must, however, illuminate the action for the audience.

### Costume

Costume reflects character and is also important in establishing the time period of this play. Key features of the female students' costumes include ankle-length skirts, button boots, boaters and bloomers. The male

### Exam tip

Make sure that you know how different lighting effects are created and use the correct words to describe them. Do not write about 'dark lighting' but about how you would **suggest** that it is dark through your use of lighting effects.

students would wear formal trousers and jackets with white, wing-collared shirts. The lecturers would wear black academic gowns and servants, such as Minnie, would wear Victorian black and white uniforms. Billy's costume would immediately identify him as working class.

Tess, Maeve, Celia and Carolyn arrive at Girton.

The male students at Trinity (Act 2, Scene 8).

## Sound

Live or recorded sound and/or music can capture mood and create atmosphere. The play opens with the arrival of the students at Cambridge railway station: the sound of trains, hissing of steam and excited chatter of arriving students creates an engaging opening to the play. Sound effects might punctuate the action, for example, recorded voices of unseen students playing the card game in Act 2, Scene 8 or ambient sound in the night-time orchard to establish the time and place. Other sound effects can be used to signify the atmosphere of Cambridge – distant church bells or birdsong. Occasional sounds are indicated in the text – the doorbell at the shop or the crash of Tess's bicycle. The sound designer might include music to suggest the period or to underscore scene transitions.

## Activity ?

Act 2, Scene 11 demands many sound effects to create both the excitement and the danger of the voting day. Read this scene from the viewpoint of the sound designer. How could you create these sound effects? Would you add any sounds other than those suggested in the text? How would your use of sound enhance the production for an audience?

## *Dr Korczak's Example* by David Greig

### Historical context

The play is set during the Second World War in Warsaw, Poland, in Dr Korczak's ghetto orphanage for Jewish children. In September 1939, Nazi Germany had invaded Poland; this triggered the outbreak of the war when Britain, France and other commonwealth countries declared war on Germany. Warsaw had the largest Jewish settlement in Europe and over the next few months Jews were relentlessly persecuted. They were forced to do manual work, regardless of their profession, their bank accounts were closed and their houses and businesses taken from them. Jewish children were removed from schools and all Jews over the age of 12 had to wear a Star of David armband. The synagogues were closed and Jewish prayers forbidden. In 1940, all Jews were forced to live in a walled area, of about a square mile, within the city. It was known as the Warsaw Ghetto and Jews who tried to leave it were shot. They were allowed meagre rations and many Jews died of starvation. The Nazis planned to exterminate all Jews and several concentration camps were established in places such as Auschwitz and Treblinka, where Jews were put to death in gas chambers.

Dr Janusz Korczak, born in 1878, was a Polish-Jewish children's author and paediatrician. As early as the 1930s he wrote about children's rights and holistic education. He was passionate about the rights of marginalised children and in 1911 he built an orphanage for Jewish children in Warsaw. It was run as a children's republic with its own parliament, court and newspaper. In 1940 Korczak's orphanage was moved into the Warsaw Ghetto and in August 1942 German soldiers collected the staff and orphans to take them to the concentration camp in Treblinka. Many people offered Korczak an opportunity to escape but he turned them all down. He stayed with his children as they boarded the trains and died with them.

Memorial to Dr Janusz Korczak in Israel.

### Taking it further

Find out more about the conditions in the Warsaw Ghetto; look for images to help you to understand the world of the play. Look on the internet for the education pack that accompanied the Unicorn Theatre's production. This provides some very useful information.

Read the final scene of the play again – these are the words of the United Nations Convention Rights of the Child (UNCRC), which was based on Dr Korczak's work. Find out more about the details of the UNCRC.

## Contemporary and performance context

David Greig's play was first performed in May 2001 in Scottish schools. The story had to be told with a small number of performers because it was touring schools. Grieg considered how he could represent the children of the orphanage and what they suffered. At the time his four-year-old daughter was playing with her toys and creating characters from objects such as toy animals or furniture. These objects did not move and she did not use funny voices. This was the inspiration for the dolls as Korczak's orphans because it forced the audience to inhabit the dolls imaginatively. The use of dolls as the orphans is an important feature of this play. Greig aimed to encapsulate both the horror of the Nazi treatment of the Jews and the idealism of Dr Korczak. He chose to set the play in the Warsaw Ghetto in the days leading up to their eviction to Treblinka. The character of Adzio was created after Greig read Dr Korczak's diary account of expelling a boy from the orphanage: the boy's violence in the ghetto was bringing the police to the orphanage and endangering other children. Adzio also provides a contrast to Dr Korczak's idealism and poses the question about how we respond in the face of injustice: with aggression like Adzio or by appealing to people's innate goodness. Greig decided that this was the central theme of his play. Today our newspapers and TV screens are often filled with images of similarly oppressed groups escaping tyranny and torture. These children do not have the rights that Dr Korczak or the United Nations envisaged. Although the play is a story about terrible events from history, there is a new, similar history being played out in many parts of the world today. *Dr Korczak's Example* also has another message for modern audiences: how do we treat each other in this self-centred and materialistic world?

## The story of *Dr Korczak's Example*

The actor, who then becomes Dr Korczak, sets the scene: we are told that it is 1942 in Warsaw, Poland, in Dr Korczak's orphanage for bereft children in a Jewish ghetto. Dr Korczak is introduced as a kind, trusting and caring man who sees the best in everyone. Adzio is introduced to the audience and he initially decides to identify with a fly, giving 'Fly' as his name. Adzio is uncooperative and offensive; he struggles to adapt to Dr Korczak's kind and humane world. Despite Adzio's anger, violence and hostility, Dr Korczak accepts him. One night, when gunshots fire, Dr Korczak talks to a Nazi soldier who is not seen or heard by the audience: these types of conversations are a feature of the play. Adzio has frightened the children by telling them that the Nazis will kill them within the next two weeks.

A Christian friend, Stepan, visits offering Dr Korczak a false passport and an opportunity to escape, but he refuses to abandon the orphans. Adzio steals bread and the children's court, which judges those who break the law, finds him guilty. He does not care and shows no remorse. Dr Korczak talks to the silent soldier about justice. Adzio does not want to play in the football match that Dr Korczak arranges but after some persuasion he gets involved, though he pushes and cheats to score his goal. Another orphan, Stephanie, tries to get closer to Adzio but he resists. Dr Korczak visits Adam Cerniakov, the leader of the Jews, who runs the ghetto. He asks whether the Nazis intend to kill the children but Cerniakov assures him that they will be safe.

The children write a letter to the priest of the Christian church asking if they can visit the church gardens to see the flowers and to breathe fresh air. When Stephanie and Adzio go together to deliver the letter they dance to a street musician's tunes, share an apple that Adzio has stolen and they kiss. The priest refuses the orphans' request and Adzio becomes enraged at the injustice – they are not welcome because they are Jews. He throws stones at the church, breaking windows, and Stephanie is encouraged to join in. Dr Korczak reprimands them but Adzio argues strongly for his right to be angry. The distraught Dr Korczak once again talks to the silent soldier about justice. Adzio asks Stephanie to escape with him and to make a life in the USA: in his fantasy they go to New York, buy fast cars and live on a farm. Their relationship is now very strong but Stephanie asks for one more day to decide because she has faith that Dr Korczak will keep them safe.

A radio announcement instructs all Jews to leave the ghetto and to go to the railway yards to be transported to 'better accommodation in the east'. Cerniakov tries to save the children but is told that there will be 'no exceptions'. He commits suicide. Dr Korczak hides his diary under the floorboards before quietly gathering the orphans together and, with great dignity, leading them to the trains. He is offered freedom but again refuses to leave the children. Adzio and Stephanie hide but are discovered by the Nazi soldiers. The play ends with the actors telling how the children threw down their Star of David armbands, which covered the cobbles like a field of buttercups.

## Character

Dr Korczak was a real person whose life story and beliefs are well documented. Adzio and Stephanie represent the orphans, while other characters, such as Cerniakov, symbolise the people who tried to help Dr Korczak. The unseen soldier is a constant reminder of the Jews'

---

### Activity ?

1  Work in a group of four or five to create a series of five still images described below showing a Jewish family's eviction to the Warsaw Ghetto. Some images may not involve everyone.

   a  The family receives the order to pack up their home and leave.

   b  Reactions of the family members.

   c  Deciding to leave a treasured item behind.

   d  Leaving their home for the last time.

   e  Walking through the streets carrying their belongings.

2  Now add a headline to each image as though it appeared in a newspaper.

3  Perform the series of images and headlines to others in your class.

incarceration within the ghetto. The playwright chose to use dolls to represent the orphans and some other characters. In his introduction to this text Greig explains that the decision was partly because a large cast was not suitable for the original schools' tour, but also to encourage the audiences to visualise the personalities of dolls, thus engaging them in the issues.

Key characters and some words that can describe them:

| Dr Korczak | Idealistic  Compassionate  Gentle |
| --- | --- |
| Adzio | Wild  Troubled  Aggressive |
| Stephanie | Loyal  Responsible  Kind |
| Stepan | Realistic  Generous  Honest |
| Cerniakov | Honourable  Pragmatic  Conscientious |
| The Priest | Hypocritical  Bigoted  Weak |
| The Nazi Officer | Merciless  Cruel  Brainwashed |

## Activity ?

Look at the mind map of Stephanie on the right. The actor has chosen three words to describe her character. Below each word there is a quotation from the text to support the choice.

Choose three characters from the play and then create a mind map for each of them. Support each word with a quotation, indicating which scene the quote is from.

LOYAL
Sc 2 Stephanie repeats 'He believes' loyal to Dr
Sc 19 She apologises because she let Dr K down

STEPHANIE

RESPONSIBLE
Sc 11 speaks up for Adzio in court despite disliking him
Sc 2 in charge of taking details of new orphans
Sc 15 the 'older boys' give her the note to take to Dr K about the church gardens

KIND
Sc 7 asks Dr K what is worrying him
Sc 13 Sits with Adzio and tries to find out why he is upset

## Creating impact in a production of *Dr Korczak's Example*

The use of dolls to signify the orphans adds a moving dimension to the production. It is sobering to realise how poignant these inanimate objects can be when they are representing the vulnerable children. In Scene 24, when Dr Korczak prepares to lead his children to the concentration camp, he speaks to the dolls with great feeling as he arranges them into marching formation. The contrast of his words with the audience's knowledge of their fate has incredible impact. The scene has many elements, including the unhurried, deliberate movement of Dr Korczak as he dresses for this final journey, the measured gathering of the dolls into lines and the description of the final destination in the countryside. The use of props also has an impact, including the orphanage flag, the yellow armbands, Dr Korczak's diary. These elements combine to give this scene an overwhelming and powerful effect on the audience.

### Activity ?

If possible, collect a number of rag dolls or alternatively use pieces of materials and elastic bands to create 'dolls'. Read Scene 24 from the stage directions *Dr Korczak prepares himself* to *and hides it under the floorboards*. Work in pairs, taking it in turns to play Dr Korczak and be the director. Rehearse the scene in different ways until you agree on the version that will have the most pathos. Remember that, in playing this scene, you could use dolls to represent the orphans being helped.

### Performing a role in *Dr Korczak's Example*

In your exam you will be asked to interpret an extract from the play. Some questions will concern your approach to playing a character, some will ask you to think from the point of view of a designer and some will require you to comment on how a director would work with an actor to realise a performance. The question below refers to Adzio in Scene 18, where he and Stephanie take the children's letter to the priest; he becomes angry and breaks the church windows.

### Exam-style question

Adzio is the most aggressive character in the orphanage. As a director, discuss how the performer playing the role might demonstrate his aggression in the extract and in the play as a whole.

You must consider:
- voice
- physicality
- stage directions and stage space. **(12 marks)**

### Exam tip

Always read the question carefully. This question requires your answer to refer to the extract and to the whole play. To gain full marks you must give reasons for your decisions and include other examples from elsewhere in the play.

# Section A Bringing texts to life

In your answer you might include:

**Voice**: Short phrases spoken sharply, e.g. 'What? Helping Jews?'; hostile tone, sneering at the priest 'You fat toad'; measured, deliberate pace and low menacing tone on 'I hope the Germans get you' with a stress on 'you'.

**Physicality**: Advancing towards the priest 'No you're not'; mimicking a fat toad on a riverbank – sticking out stomach, slumping onto the floor (*plopped down*) miming catching flies; being intimidating by moving behind the priest speaking over his shoulder into his face on 'They've got an office ...'

**Stage space/directions**: Hunched shoulders, walking quickly ahead of Stephanie when *He ignores her*; energy and violence in the mime of *hurling* stone; eye contact with Stephanie and a pause as his stillness invites her to throw when *he gives her a stone*.

## Taking it further

Research the theories of Bertolt Brecht. Make a list of his key techniques, then examine *Dr Korczak's Example* and identify how Greig uses Brecht's strategies in this play.

## Activity ?

In a group or as a whole class use conscience alley to explore whether the soldier follows orders because his fear of the Nazis is more powerful than his human goodness.

## Taking it further

Look online for a video interview with James Button about his designs for the Unicorn Theatre.

## Working as the director of *Dr Korczak's Example*

The play is written in a **Brechtian** structure. This type of theatre is based on the theories of the German playwright Bertolt Brecht. He wanted his audiences to remain objective and distant from emotional involvement so that they could make considered and rational judgements. This style of theatre suits plays where there is a political or moral message. *Dr Korczak's Example* employs many Brechtian devices, such as direct address to the audience, narration, symbolic use of props and episodic scenes.

In Scene 10 the director might work with the performer playing Adzio on physical skills. Adzio's outburst and aggression at the football match must be conveyed in a small space with the dolls representing the other players. The actor playing Adzio can communicate that he is watching the 'match' before bursting into the space and taking the ball. His antagonism needs to be conveyed physically in very few lines. Directors will always investigate the text in various ways during the rehearsal process.

Dr Korczak often speaks to the unseen Nazi soldier: this Brechtian device enables the audience to share what Dr Korczak is thinking and feeling. In Scene 18 Dr Korczak asks the soldier 'What do you see ... inside your own head?' A director could use the activity on the left to explore this question.

## Working as a designer on *Dr Korczak's Example*

The **set design** creates the world of the play. Initial decisions will involve the shape of the stage space, the position of entrances and exits and the mood and atmosphere of each scene. **Props** are also extremely important in a production of this play. Props can be used to signify locations in the minimalist, symbolic set, for example, the football, the clipboard and the apples. James Button's design for the Unicorn Theatre was a timeless, harsh world where the action was surrounded by a metal fence. There were no soft edges. Beyond the fence, boxes were piled up, which were symbolic of the displacement of the orphans. Some of these boxes were brought into the space and used to create locations and seating. Faceless dolls represented the orphans. Miriam Nabarro's design for Manchester Royal Exchange used suitcases to signify the transience of the ghetto with tiny pairs of shoes surrounding the action.

## Activity **?**

Write the title in the centre of a large piece of paper. Draw 25 lines of different lengths from the title, each one representing a scene. At the end of the lines write the numbers 1–25. For each scene write the location, e.g. 3 – Korczak's office, 8 – canteen, 18 – church. Below each title write two or three ways the set denotes the location, e.g. office – desk, chair, papers.

## Costume

Costume design builds belief in the characters and the story using instantly recognisable items of clothing. For example, a long grey, buttoned coat and helmet for the Nazi soldier, the orphans in simple ragged skirts, or worn patched trousers, waistcoats and shirts with caps or headscarves and boots. By contrast, Dr Korczak might wear a black suit, a clean, white shirt and a hat to go outside. As Korczak is a real person the designer can research his appearance. He always wore round spectacles. The yellow armbands with the Star of David are also important items of costume.

## Lighting

*Dr Korczak's Example* is usually performed on a minimalist set so lighting is extremely important to establish atmosphere and location. There are no lighting cues in the text so the lighting designer will need to investigate the play to establish the sources of light, the time of day and the atmosphere of the location. Bright, straw-coloured light can be used to communicate sunshine in the playground, whereas a cold, blue light, with areas of shadow, can convey the threatening atmosphere of the ghetto at night. Lighting will also focus attention on specific areas of the stage space, for example, Dr Korczak's office in Scene 3.

## Sound

Sound also has an important function in creating mood and location. The play opens with a burst of playground noise punctuated by a siren and martial music. These sounds immediately communicate the tension between the innocence of the orphans and the oppression of the Nazi control. The flies buzzing in Scenes 2 and 8 are symbolic of the ease with which life is destroyed. Sound frequently communicates anger or oppression – gunshots, threatening radio announcements, sirens, the smashing of the church window. Music can be part of the action, for example, from the street musician who Adzio and Stephanie meet. Music might be used to create atmosphere or to link scenes.

## Taking it further

Find out about the clothing worn by the Jews in the 1940s ghetto. Look in the library or on the internet for photographs from that period.

# Section A: Bringing texts to life

**Question (a)(i)**

*There are specific choices in this extract for performers.*

*You are going to play Lloyd. Explain two ways you would use physical skills to play this character in this extract.*

**(4 marks)**

These are sections from student answers based on an extract from **Blue Stockings** by Jessica Swale, Act 2, Scene 6 from 'What would you do with a degree anyway?' to the end of the scene.

## Student A

Lloyd is a bigoted and somewhat arrogant man, therefore if I were playing the role I would hold the centre of the stage space, controlling the early part of the scene. This would indicate that I saw myself as superior and had no respect for the women. When Lloyd 'Explodes' my fury would be punctuated by slamming my hand down on the shop counter on 'Listen!', turning sharply to face Carolyn, engaging her with blazing eyes to intimidate her. During the speech I would move abruptly between Tess and Carolyn on key lines, each movement a threat, but otherwise remain still. This stillness gives Lloyd power.

> The paragraph gives two clear and relevant examples of the use of physical skills with specific reasons for these choices. Further points indicate exact moments with precise references to the extract. The answer goes on to give finer details of the expression in Lloyd's eyes and his movement and gesture.

## Overall commentary

This is a strong response because:

- it responds precisely to the question
- examples of physical skills are justified using subject-specific language
- it shows a depth of understanding of the character and how the performance skills communicate the role.

## Student B

If I were performing Lloyd in this extract, I would move across the stage as though I was in charge rather than a customer in the shop. I would not look at the two girls because I see them as inferior. When I get really angry I would push the material off the counter and then move close to Carolyn screaming into her face. In the long speech I would pace about stopping now and then to confront the women.

> The answer opens by referencing one movement and links this to the character's attitude. It goes on to suggest how the character pushes the material from the counter and makes a point about moving very close to Carolyn's face. The final sentence makes a general comment about movement.

## Overall commentary

This is an average response because:

- it answers the question without the flair of a confident response
- examples of physical skills are evident and there is occasional use of subject-specific language
- it shows some understanding of character without linking specifically to communicating the role.

## Student C

I would play Lloyd by being angry with the girl in the shop because she says she can be a doctor. I would stamp around a lot when I was angry. When I say the long speech I would walk up and down and throw some things off the counter then I would walk around and not stop until I was finished because I don't want her to be a doctor.

> The answer makes a basic point about the character's anger and suggests one action. A further comment is made regarding movement but suggestions are not supported by detail or references to the extract.

## Overall commentary

This is a weak response because:

- it is largely narrative with basic understanding
- the answer is underdeveloped with no use of subject-specific vocabulary
- the response lacks analysis or an understanding of how the use of the skill might communicate.

**Question (a)(ii)**

*There are specific choices in this extract for performers.*

*You are going to play the Mayor. As a performer, give three suggestions of how you would use performance skills to engage the audience in this extract.*

*You must provide a reason for each suggestion.*

**(6 marks)**

These are sections from student answers based on an extract from **Government Inspector** by Nikolai Gogol in a version by David Harrower, Act 2 from 'If you're a little short of funds' to 'Really very rare'.

## Student A

The Mayor is an oily individual and at this point in the play he thinks Khlestakov is high-ranking. I would wring my hands and lean towards Khlestakov when offering 'funds'. This would lower the Mayor's status while also playing on the dramatic irony and mistaken identity to engage the audience. My voice would have a nervous high pitch with a fawning tone to add to the farce of the confusion.

> The first paragraph demonstrates an excellent understanding of the character and gives very well detailed examples of the use of performance skills and references the audience response.

When speaking the asides to the audience, I would use a sarcastic vocal tone, sharply contrasting to my earlier grovelling voice. I would move to a point very close to the audience speaking directly to individuals. The audience will feel part of the action, yet superior, as they know that Khlestakov is merely a clerk.

> The second paragraph uses detailed subject-specific language and also connects with the audience.

When the Mayor asks Khlestakov to stay at his own house, I would speak with an obviously insincere vocal tone and make exaggerated flamboyant gestures on 'I wonder, would ... No, No' and 'I was going to ask if ....' This ridiculous wheedling will amuse the audience. The line 'I hate obsequiousness and fawning and all that ...' coming almost immediately afterwards, will have even more impact.

> The third paragraph links voice, movement and gesture using subject-specific language. The use of performance skills is linked with clear reasoning and exact references to the text.

## Overall commentary

This is a strong response because:

- it gives three examples supported by reasons and locates them precisely in the extract
- there is confident use of subject-specific language
- it shows an excellent understanding of how performance skills reflect character and communicate with an audience.

## Student B

If I was going to play the Mayor in this extract, I would speak with a slow pace and try to sound in awe because Khlestakov is a Government Inspector. My voice would be smarmy, as I want to get him on my side and make him think that everything in the town is good. When I tell him about the lovely room in my house I would try to sound very enthusiastic about it because I want to impress him.

The moments when I talk to the audience I would sound very different, especially when I call him a 'Tosser' – the audience would find this funny because they know that he is not an Inspector.

In the scene I would turn to the audience and look at them when I speak to them. This would mean that they knew what I really felt and that I was only pretending to be to be pleasant.

> The first paragraph addresses the use of vocal skills and shows an understanding of character and situation.

> The second paragraph refers to the engagement of the audience but without use of subject-specific detail.

> The third paragraph also shows an understanding of the importance of engagement with the audience but lacks detail.

## Overall commentary

This is an average response because:

- the student addresses performance skills
- examples of physical skills are discussed and there is use of subject-specific language
- it shows a knowledge of the character and an awareness of the intended audience response.

## Student C

If I was performing the role of the Mayor in this extract, I would use performance skills to try to get the man who they think is the Government Inspector to take some money as a bribe. I would also use my voice and my movement and my eyes when I ask him to come to my house because I don't want him think that I am making it bad for the people who live in the town. He is not an inspector but I don't know that now. I will use these performance skills to show my role when I do this on the stage to the audience.

> The answer repeats many of the phrases from the question and identifies some performance skills without giving specific detail. The response is a simple narrative of some events in the extract but the answer lacks analysis or understanding of how performance skills might be used to communicate with the audience.

## Overall commentary

This is a weak response because:

- it is largely a narrative with some references to the question
- it is underdeveloped and lacks specific detail.

**Question (b)(i)**

*There are specific choices in this extract for a director.*

*As a director, discuss how you would use one of the production elements below to bring this extract to life for your audience. You should make reference to the context in which the text was created and performed. Choose one of the following:*

- costume
- staging
- props/stage furniture.

**(9 marks)**

These are sections from student answers based on an extract from **An Inspector Calls** by J.B. Priestley, Act 2 from 'She'd come to you for assistance' to the end of the act.

## Student A

My costume designs would reflect the post-Edwardian era, the Birling's upper-middle-class status and the fact that the Birling family is dressed for a dinner party. The play, originally performed in 1946, is set in 1912. Priestley wanted to alert the audience to the way wealthy people cared only about themselves: this was true in 1912 but the post-war elite had similar attitudes. The remnants of the dinner would be visible on the set: a table with crystal glasses, white napkins and silver cutlery. A chandelier hangs above the table.

My costume colour scheme would be tones of black, grey and white with sparkling beads to mirror the glasses and chandelier, a constant reminder of wealth. Birling would wear a black tail-coat with a white winged collared shirt because they had been at a formal dinner. This also indicates his social status. He may have loosened his tie or removed his coat at this stage in the play as the questioning is becoming intense. The two women, Sybil Birling and her daughter Sheila, would contrast. Sybil is a mature lady so I would costume her in a high-necked, full-length dress made from taffeta with a black lace overdress and a train falling at the back. The dress would be appliqued with jet beading to indicate the wealth of the family. Sheila is a younger woman and she would embrace newer styles. Her floor-length cream silk dress would have a narrower silhouette, tapering towards the ankles and a lower cowl style neckline. It would be decorated with small pearls. This shows that Sheila is also wealthy but she wears more up-to-date fashions and enjoys shopping for clothes. Both women would wear earrings and necklaces of expensive jewels: this links with the glittering of the beads and the set details. At this moment in the play Sheila is becoming distressed so her hair may be dishevelled: Sybil remains confident and defiant and would continue to appear immaculate.

The Inspector is from a different class and possibly from a different world. He would wear shades of grey to suggest both class and the otherworldly nature of the character. He wears a dark grey woollen overcoat over a charcoal suit with a white shirt and grey tie. He wears or carries a black hat.

*The first paragraph makes several points about the context of the play and the intentions of the playwright. It goes on to reference the other design elements and this shows a secure knowledge of the design process.*

*The second paragraph gives specific details of the costume design for Sybil and Sheila Birling, and makes points about contemporary fashion, linking them to the age difference between the characters. The answer uses specific language to describe texture, shape and detail. Further points are made to the extract, and to the meaning and context of the scene.*

*The third paragraph explores how the costume design for Inspector Goole might set him apart from the other characters.*

## Overall commentary

This is a strong response because:

- it demonstrates a secure knowledge and understanding of the costume designer's role
- there are specific references to the extract and to the wider context of the play
- the use of technical and subject-specific terminology clearly communicates ideas.

## Student B

My costume designs for this extract would show that the Birling family are very rich. The play was written in 1946 but J.B. Priestley set it in 1912. The Birlings have been at a dinner in their house and they are dressed up in fine clothes. I want to show that they have a great amount of money to buy clothes. Mr Birling is the head of the house and he is important in the town. He wears a dinner suit that is black and it has a long coat. Mrs Birling is dressed for an engagement party for her daughter. She wears a long dress with a lot of decorations, like beads and lace. This tells the audience that she is rich. Sheila is younger and she would wear an evening dress. She would be dressed up because she had just got engaged. Her dress is made of satin and it shines in the lights. She wears a diamond necklace.

Inspector Goole might be a ghost but the family think he is real. He does not wear rich clothes. He would be wearing an overcoat that is brown and very plain. He has a suit and a shirt and tie on and he wears a hat.

> The first paragraph makes a point about the status of the Birling family and the circumstances of the extract. This is followed by two specific examples of the Birling's wealth and the intentions of the costume design. There are details about the style, material and decoration of the costumes for the female characters.

> The second paragraph refers to the enigma of the Inspector and suggests some costume ideas.

### Overall commentary

This is an average response because:

- it shows sound understanding of the role of the costume designer
- it answers the question with effective use of subject-specific language
- examples are supported by reasons and related to the text.

## Student C

The play is about being rich and not caring much about other people when it was written and it is put in a different time from then. If I was doing the costumes for this extract, I would dress Sheila and Sybil in long expensive dresses with decoration on them. They are rich and important in the town and there has been a dinner party. Mr Birling would wear a man's suit and it would be black because at that time when the men had a dinner they wore those suits. The Inspector has come to the house to ask questions about a girl who has died. He was not at the dinner party. Now he is asking Mrs Birling about when she didn't give any money to Eva Smith. He is going to wear a coat because he has not long come in and hasn't taken it off.

> The paragraph makes a point about the style of costumes during this era. It makes a point about the status of the family and how costume could reflect character. The final sentences are purely narrative mentioning only the Inspector's coat.

### Overall commentary

This is a weak response because:

- it lacks focus but shows some understanding of the function of costume
- there is occasional use of subject-specific vocabulary
- the response loses focus and becomes narrative in the final section.

**Question (b)(i)**

*There are specific choices in this extract for a director.*

*As a director, discuss how you would use one of the production elements below to bring this extract to life for your audience. You should make reference to the context in which the text was created and performed. Choose one of the following:*

- costume
- staging
- props/stage furniture.

**(9 marks)**

These are sections from student answers based on an extract from **DNA** by Dennis Kelly, Act 2 Scene 3 from 'he wouldn't speak to us' to 'Say something Phil'.

## Student A

The play's settings move between four outdoor locations: street to a field, a hill and a wood. I would stage this extract in a small studio space in a thrust setting with the audience raised on three sides and the stage action at floor level. This would create a claustrophobic and intense atmosphere. The setting is a wood, which would be implied with back projection of dense trees with a clearing of rough grassland to the front of the image. The stage space would be lit with dappled leaves, bringing the action into the woodland. There are four entrances: up stage right (USR) and USL and down right (DR) and DL via the audience. The effect of this staging is that the audience feel as though they are in the wood and possibly complicit in the action. The play is about peer pressure, written for and performed by teenagers: the proximity of the audience would force them to question the morals of Adam's treatment.

The first paragraph details the style of staging, references how the location would be created, and indicates the entrances and exits. There is clear reasoning for these choices. Further details include use of back projection and lighting effects. The final part of the paragraph refers to the original performance and links with the intended effect on an audience.

There is an atmosphere of menace, which would be created by Adam's appearance and by the obvious lack of care of the teenagers: Phil sits silently and apart towards the front of the stage area on a battered beer crate. His isolation and refusal to communicate suggests his power.

The second paragraph discusses the mood and atmosphere, suggesting ways in which the staging creates menace. A further point discusses how Phil is seated and discusses the power of his silence.

I would stage the moment when Brian eats mud in the centre of the space with the others grouped behind him so that the whole audience can see it. Brian is losing his sanity because of the pressure and the audience would feel empathy for him.

The third paragraph refers to a specific moment in the extract and links the staging decision to the intended impact on the audience.

## Overall commentary

This is a strong response because:

- it makes specific points about staging with precise examples from the extract
- there is consistently effective use of subject-specific terminology
- the answer addresses the key points from the question and justifies the choices.

## Student B

All the scenes in the play are outdoors in different places. This scene takes place in a wood so the staging must make the audience realise that it is a wood. There would be a projection of trees on the back wall of the stage so it looks like a wood. The audience sit round the space on chairs and the stage is flat. They can all see what is happening because they are very close. The actors will come in and out through gaps in the audience.

Phil sits down all the way through and he does not speak. The teenagers thought that Adam was dead but he is alive. This might be a shock to the audience. The others do not seem to care that he is hurt and dirty.

The play is about teenagers and it was written for them. It is about peer pressure and that is why the audience, who might also be teenagers, are sat close to it. They should feel guilty if they have done any bullying themselves.

The first paragraph makes a point about the various locations in the play and suggests projection to convey the wood. Further points are made about the configuration of the audience and the entrances and exits without comment to justify the choices.

The second paragraph notes that Phil sits silently and explains that Adam's appearance is a shock to the teenagers and the audience. A further comment notes that the gang does not care about Adam.

The final paragraph mentions the context of the play and suggests how the chosen staging could give the play impact.

## Overall commentary

This is an average response because:

- it balances the different elements of the staging logically
- it uses subject-specific language with understanding
- there is an understanding of the context of the play and audience involvement.

## Student C

This scene is in a wood but the theatre is not a wood so I would make it to look like a wood. The wood is done with putting a picture of the trees on the back wall. The audience is around the part where the actors are acting. They are very close so they would all be able to see. People come in from the audience in the gaps. The play is for teenagers and the bullying that they do sometimes. It was done for the competition in London and then at a theatre. Phil is sitting on the floor and he does not say anything at all. Adam is meant to be dead but he is not dead any more.

The answer begins by identifying the location of the scene and goes on to suggest the use of projected images but there is no use of subject-specific language. It makes a point about the position of the audience and entrances/exit and makes reference to the original production and to the theme. The final section is a narrative description of events in the extract.

## Overall commentary

This is a weak response because:

- it makes basic points in reference to the question but lacks structure
- it uses basic subject-specific language without detail or analysis
- it has become a simple narrative description.

# Preparing for your exam

### Question (b)(ii)

*There are specific choices in this extract for a director.*

*Malvolio is an important comic character in the play. As a director, discuss how the performer playing this role might make the audience laugh in this extract and the complete play. You must consider:*

- *voice*
- *physicality*
- *stage directions and stage space.*

**(12 marks)**

These are sections from student answers based on an extract from **Twelfth Night** by William Shakespeare, Act 2, Scene 5 from 'What employment have we here?' to 'I will do everything that thou wilt have me'.

## Student A

Malvolio is a figure of fun throughout the play: he is pompous and considers himself of high status because he is Olivia's steward. As a director, I would set this persona up in the early part of the play – for example in Act 1 Olivia refers to him as 'sick of self-love' suggesting that he is vain and self-centred. In his early entrances Malvolio would speak with an affected voice and assume an upright posture. Leading up to this extract Malvolio has aggravated Sir Toby, Maria and Feste by reprimanding them for making too much noise and telling them that they 'gabble like tinkers' (low-class vagrants). I would direct Malvolio to look down his nose at them with dismissive gestures and speak in a curt tone of voice.

I want to exploit the dramatic irony of the situation in the extract and enlist the audience in delighting in Malvolio's downfall. In this extract Malvolio is talking to himself, and the audience are 'overhearing' – as are the characters hiding in the box tree. When he first reads the letter Malvolio would trace the letters with his fingers and show that he does not understand the double-entendre of 'c's u's and t's': he would stress these letters saying them slowly so that the audience makes the connection. When he touches the sealing wax it is still 'soft' and sticks to his fingers – he would grimace while trying to wipe it off on his clothes.

Malvolio would utter a gasp on 'If this should be thee, Malvolio' to show shock that his mistress would show him affection. He would then very slowly draw himself up to his full height and puff out his chest with pride. The obvious nature of this response would amuse the audience, as they know the letter is forged. The riddle MOAI would initially be pronounced as one word – perhaps sounding like 'Miaow', which would make him sound ridiculous and therefore draw a laugh from the audience. As he reads the letter aloud he would wander across the stage space stopping very close to the box tree. The characters hiding would pop up behind him but he does not see them. This would create a moment of visual humour. As he reads the lines about greatness he would stretch to appear taller and taller with a self-satisfied facial expression. Malvolio would mime wearing the cross garters and move across the stage as though modelling them. On the line 'I will be point device the very man' he would strike an exaggerated pose, facing the audience, to demonstrate his new position as the perfect man for Olivia.

Later in the play he becomes a sad character, imprisoned, tormented and teased so his posture and voice would be less superior. When Olivia confirms that the letter was not by her hand he would be subdued, downcast. His final exit is slow with his shoulders drooping, and by this time the audience have sympathy for Malvolio.

---

The first paragraph makes two points about Malvolio's character and goes on to discuss his function in the play. There are two points about how Malvolio would use vocal and physical skills to convey character in the earlier scenes in the play. There are well-argued reasons in support of these choices.

The second paragraph identifies the dramatic irony of the scene and makes a point about engaging the audience. Further points are made about the use of voice, movement, gesture and facial expression with references to the effect on the audience and reasons for the decisions. Each point is supported with reference to the text.

The third paragraph makes two points about Malvolio's voice and movement with detailed comments about the audience reaction. Another two points about physicality pinpoint the moments in the text and suggest possible audience responses.

The final paragraph discusses changes in Malvolio's character in the later stages of the play with examples of how performance skills would reflect character and evoke the audience's sympathy.

## Overall commentary

This is a strong response because:

- it is detailed and focused on the question
- it demonstrates a balanced knowledge of how performance skills communicate with an audience
- examples are well developed and support the points.

## Student B

Malvolio is the funniest character in the play and in this extract he is almost speaking a monologue to the audience as the other characters do not speak to him directly. Malvolio is talking to himself in the hearing of the audience. When he picks up the letter and says 'My Life!' I want the performer to use a high-pitched voice that almost sounds like a squeak: the audience would find this funny because it makes him sound camp. When he reads the letter I would ask him to stress the 'c','u' and 't' because this is rude and I want the audience to laugh at it. When he reads the letter his voice would be excited when he thinks about what it means. He should sound puzzled when he tries to work out what MAOI means: I would suggest that he scratches his head and frowns.

Malvolio's movements would show that he is comic. When he picks up the letter and touches the wax it is soft and it goes on his fingers. He would wipe if off and pull a face. When he is reading the letter he would walk up and down as though he was thinking about what it all means. Malvolio would mime wearing the cross garters and do a little walk as if he was modelling them and when he thinks that he is the man in the letter he would do a pose.

Malvolio would use the stage space by walking up and down with pauses when he speaks about the letter. I would ask him to move close to the box tree as he was reading the riddle and bump into it. The hiding characters speak but he does not see them. This would be funny because the audience know that they are there. He would finish the scene by smiling a big false smile because Olivia has told him in the letter that when he sees her she wants him to smile. Malvolio would walk off facing the audience and smiling. This would be amusing because it is false and a bit silly.

In the rest of the play Malvolio is pompous and a bit arrogant and he thinks he is better than everyone else. This scene happens because Sir Toby Belch is angry with him and he wants to teach him a lesson. Malvolio is a bit of a figure of fun in the play.

> The first paragraph makes the point that Malvolio's speech is essentially a monologue with the audience overhearing. It goes on to make clear points about the use of voice with examples from the text.

> The second paragraph makes points about movement, facial expression and gesture, and links these to the audience response.

> The third paragraph makes three points about the use of stage space and facial expression, relating these to the audience reaction.

> The final paragraph makes basic points about Malvolio in the complete play but this is largely narrative and is not related to the rest of the answer.

## Overall commentary

This is an average answer because:

- it makes relevant points in answer to all the components in the question but lacks the flair of a stronger response
- it is a generally balanced answer and uses subject-specific language in a logical way
- there is a sound understanding of the way a director would communicate ideas to the audience but there is only basic reference to the complete play.

**Question (c)**

*There are specific choices in this extract for designers.*

*Discuss how you would use **one** design element to enhance the production of this extract for the audience. Choose one of the following:*

- *set*
- *lighting*
- *sound.*

**(14 marks)**

These are sections from student answers based on an extract from **1984** by Robert Icke and Duncan Macmillan, Two Minutes Hate from *A klaxon sounds* to 'Two minutes Hate is over, comrades'.

## Student A

Sound is very important in this play because there are very many sound effects in the text. Sound shows what is happening and it can have an effect on the audience; sometimes the sound is very loud and intense. I would want the sound in the production to make the audience feel uneasy and sometimes want to put their fingers in their ears. The actors would make some sounds, like when they are chanting and screaming at the screen and other sounds are recorded and played through the speakers in the theatre. 1984 is about a society where no one has any freedom and in this section a person is being shot because they don't agree with Big Brother. It is called Two Minutes Hate because this happens all the time and the people have to watch the screen and join in or else they might be shot too.

> The first paragraph makes three points about the role of sound in theatre and in this production in particular. This is followed by references to the intended effect on the audience. A further point describes the use of recorded and live sound. The final part of the paragraph makes a comment about the meaning of the play and goes on to locate the extract in the plot.

The sound of the klaxon would be very loud as it tells the people that they have to stop what they are doing and go to the screen. I would record the metal sound with the grinding and that would be played through the speakers as well. When everybody is shouting at the Thought Criminal that would be the actors not the sound person but when there is a sheep bleating that would be a sound effect.

> The second paragraph begins with two examples of sound effects and a basic description of how they would be created. The paragraph ends with an undeveloped reference to different uses of live or recorded sound.

The gunshot is made with a sound effect. Sometimes in a play when an actor shoots the gun on the stage it is done with a fake gun that fires blanks. In this play the gun is on the screen so it would come from the speakers. When Winston has to have his voice made louder to go over the top of the shouting he would wear a microphone on his clothes and the sound team in the lighting box would operate it.

> The third paragraph mentions two further examples of sound in the extract. There is a straightforward explanation of how and why the gunshot sound is created. The final comment explains how Winston's voice is amplified.

## Overall commentary

This is an average response because:

- it is balanced and shows an understanding of the function of sound in the play
- it uses subject-specific terminology and shows an understanding of how the sound enhances the production for the audience
- examples are used effectively to support reasons.

## Student B

1984 was described by one critic as 'an assault on the senses'. Sound design is integral to the meaning of the play, highlighting the oppression of the citizens of Oceania. My concept for the sound design is that it should be used aggressively to create the world of 1984, unnerving the audience and keeping them on edge as they anticipate the next disturbing sound. The 'Two Minutes Hate' encapsulates the totalitarian control of the regime, and the sound must reflect both the fear of the victims and the orchestrated responses of the citizens.

*The first paragraph clearly outlines the sound design ideas for the whole play and for the extract. There is reference to the intended impact on the audience.*

This section opens with the piecing sound of a klaxon. This sound is associated with a public warning: it is a call to action and as such would be loud. The klaxon would be ear shattering and I would create an effect that echoes around the theatre, calling not only the people of Oceania but also the audience to attention. This sound would continue until everyone was assembled at the screen and then seamlessly the slow countdown would begin. There is no silence. The countdown would play through four speakers surrounding the audience, coming from everywhere in the theatre. The countdown increases in volume until it is almost too loud to bear. The following 'moment of silence' provides a contrast. This 'moment' will last for another 10 seconds accentuating the effect of the 'horrifically loud screaming grinding metallic noise' that then explodes at full volume. This effect is created by layering different sounds to create a richer texture: the grinding sound would be a low pitched metallic scraping that sets the audience's teeth on edge, while the screaming would be a high-pitched whistle that disturbs the audience in a contrasting way. The abrupt stop and silence gives a moment of relief before the audience is faced with a disturbing visual image.

*The second paragraph explores three sound effects; it gives precise details of how and why they are created and the desired effect on the audience. There are logical reasons supported by specific textual references.*

I would use the actors' voices to enhance the live sound – for the shouting, roaring, raging cheers and chanting – by recording, augmenting and distorting the voices so that they can be played electronically, amplified and accompanying the live sound of the actors' voices. For example, 'the crowd roar and scream at the screen with increasing volume and ferocity'. This would enable the sound to become louder and harsher and have a jarring effect that almost deafens the audience. When the crowd 'bleat' the sound would initially come only from the actors' voices: I would then bring in recorded sounds of sheep imperceptibly so that the audience gradually becomes aware that the volume and texture are changing.

*The third paragraph makes specific points about the use of recorded sound to augment live sound throughout the extract. There is a relevant and detailed explanation of intentions, how this would be accomplished, using subject-specific terminology and supported by textual reference linked to the effect on the audience.*

Winston's voice amplified, over the 'raging' noise of the crowd, would be achieved with a radio mike attached to Winston's costume. He would speak normally and the sound operator would increase the volume so that his voice is played through the speakers. The gunshot would be a recorded effect that reverberates around the theatre, again shockingly loud. The final klaxon is not amplified and does not echo: it suggests that the 'world' now returns to normal.

*The final paragraph makes three points about the sound at the end of the extract. It distinguishes between recorded sound effects and amplification of the actor's voice. There is an explanation of the meaning created by the difference in the sound of the klaxon at the end of the extract.*

## Overall commentary

This is a strong answer because:

- it demonstrates a very good understanding of the design element and of the play
- it uses precise subject-specific language and references to the text and makes interconnected points
- the audience is central to the response.

**Question (c)**

*There are specific choices in this extract for designers.*

*Discuss how you would use* **one** *design element to enhance the production of this extract for the audience. Choose one of the following:*

- *set*     - *lighting*     - *sound.*     **(14 marks)**

These are sections from student answers based on an extract from **Dr Korczak's Example** by David Greig, Scenes 11 and 12.

## Student A

The set I would design for this extract would be in a theatre in-the-round so that the audience is seated all around the acting space. They would be close so they would get involved with the play and the story of the Jewish orphans. The extract needs two places to be made – a courtroom and a window with a soldier outside it. When David Greig wrote the play he wanted it to be like Brecht who did not want real scenery. He thought that things should be symbols of the furniture and not to have real desks and tables and doors.

> The first paragraph identifies the style of the performance space and relates this to audience involvement. A further point links the requirements of the extract to Brecht and to the playwright.

The play is about how this good man who was a doctor helped the Jewish children but they did not escape the concentration camps. The Doctor talks to a Nazi soldier who is not ever seen by the audience. There needs to be a window but in the round that is more difficult so I would have it in one of the gaps in the audience where they come in. It gets moved when they need to go out at the end. All the desks and chairs are not real but imagined by using other objects. I would have rostra blocks like we have in our studio and you put them in different places to pretend they are desks. This would be for the court. The dolls are put on a block, not on a table or chair. When the court is over the blocks get moved and Dr Korczak stands in the gap by the window and talks to the soldier who is not there.

> The second paragraph notes the theme of the play and goes on to discuss the specific set requirements and evaluates the use of theatre in-the-round. It then details the way in which furniture can be symbolised by rostra. There is a comment about the transition to Scene 12 and its staging.

The play must make the audience think about what happened in the war to the Jews.

> The final comment refers to the theme and the intended audience response.

## Overall commentary

This is a weak response because:

- it shows some understanding of how a designer would interpret the text for an audience
- it uses some subject-specific language and there is a sense of the audience response
- it has some detail with examples that partially support the choices.

## Student B

Dr Korczak's Example is written in a Brechtian style: my set would employ the features of Brecht's thinking. The play requires multiple locations within the Ghetto. Although the majority of the action takes place in the orphanage, several scenes are located elsewhere. The first part of the extract is the children's court and in the second part Dr Korczak speaks to the Nazi soldier outside the window. It is important that the set design engages the audience in the meaning of the play. I would stage the play on a thrust stage in an intimate studio setting because the audience would be close to the action. On the rear wall there would be a screen for back projection. Entrances and exits would be from the rear of the stage and via the audience.

> The first paragraph makes a point about Brechtian design and relates this to the design concept. It goes on to identify precisely the location in the extract. Further comments pinpoint the desired effect on the audience and specify entrances and exits and how back projection will be used.

Each scene would have a title, written in legible but scrawled children's handwriting, projected onto the screen. Scene 11 is 'Adzio stands trial for stealing the bread' and Scene 12 is 'Dr Korczak talks to the soldier'. Brecht used placards and also announced the scenes: I have combined these features in this use of projection. Throughout the play black and white images would be projected onto a screen, one for each scene that appears after the title. For Scene 11 an image of Dr Korczak's court in the Warsaw orphanage and for Scene 12 an image of a Nazi soldier carrying a gun. This builds belief for the audience but does not engage them in an emotional attachment to the character. This mirrors the symbolic representation of the orphans by dolls, as suggested by David Greig.

> The second paragraph gives precise detail of the projected titles and images with clear reasons and links to the audience.

Brecht's set design was minimal and symbolic. In my design for this extract the window would be suspended from the flies and would be simply a wooden window frame. Visible behind this are crossed poles, made from broom handles, 'dressed' in a Nazi great coat and helmet with a gun over the shoulder, as if seen from behind. When Dr Korczak speaks to the soldier an overhead spotlight illuminates the symbolic figure. Desks, chairs and beds are represented by rough wooden packing cases. These can be moved and configured into different settings, representing the furniture while also reminding the audience that the children have been relocated to the Ghetto. Two cases together become the desk and others are positioned for the children, and 'dolls' to create the court. The cases are moved swiftly to the sides by the actors, in full view of the audience. The space is now empty for Dr Korczak to set up the football match before Scene 12. The design captures the minimalism of Brechtian theatre, symbolises the transience of the Jewish orphans' existence, while the projected images and the proximity of the audience engages them in the powerful meaning of the play.

> The third paragraph makes a point about minimalist and symbolic Brechtian staging and exemplifies this for the chosen design. The symbolic window and the multi-purpose packing cases are explained. Details are given as to how the items mentioned in the extract will be represented. There is a link to another design element, lighting. Finally, there is a summary of the important points with clearly defined intention for audience engagement.

## Overall commentary

This is a strong response because:

- it is well balanced with precise detail showing an understanding of the text and set design
- examples use subject-specific language showing an excellent grasp of how design creates meaning for an audience
- the response is well thought out and contains detail and focus throughout.

**Question (c)**

*There are specific choices in this extract for designers.*

*Discuss how you would use **one** design element to enhance the production of this extract for the audience. Choose one of the following:*

- *set*
- *lighting*
- *sound.*

**(14 marks)**

These are sections from student answers based on an extract from **The Crucible** by Arthur Miller, Act 4 from *Hathorne enters with Danforth and with them Cheever, Parris and Hale* to 'I confess to God and God has seen my name on this! It is enough!'

## Student A

When I am lighting this play it needs to be dark because it is in the jail at night. The people are in prison and John Proctor is in chains. He has come to see Elizabeth in the prison cell. The lighting will have to be dark until later in the scene when it gets a lot lighter and then it will be showing that it is morning. There are no real lights in the prison only the moon and it won't be very bright. I will use the lighting to show that it is going to get lighter because when the sun rises John Proctor is going to get hanged because he will not say that he is a witch. The scene is in Salem and it was a long time ago when they thought that people could be witches. It is hard to do the lighting when it is darkness because when you have to do lighting in another play it might be day or lamps are on and things.

> The answer begins by making a point about the darkness in the jail. There is a lack of clarity and the answer has little focus. It locates the scene and indicates an understanding of the lighting change during this section. The response then gives plot details and identifies problems in creating darkness on stage.

## Overall commentary

This is a weak response because:

- it tends to be mainly narrative and lacks specific focus
- it contains few examples, which only tentatively relate to the ideas
- it has little use of technical or subject-specific language.

## Student B

My lighting design for Act 4 would be to create the mood and atmosphere of the jail. It is night in the autumn of 1692 in Salem: it would be cold and stark. The lighting would evoke this environment with shadow and moonlight. There are high, barred windows at the back of the set and moonlight shines through the bars. A strong backlight is positioned behind the windows and a spotlight with a gobo of bars projects the image onto the floor of the stage. A gel in Light Steel Blue would be placed in front of the lantern to create moonlight. The lighting must, nevertheless, illuminate the actors despite the fact that the prison is dark. Dim, pale lighting would illuminate key areas of action, leaving shadowy corners and creating shadow on the faces of John and Elizabeth. By this point in the play the audience would have sympathy for Elizabeth and John Proctor: this is the first time they are seen in the jail. The lighting contributes to the audience reaction to this situation.

> The first paragraph makes points about mood, atmosphere, location and time, and links to the lighting design. Further points are made about the effect of the moonlit jail and barred windows. The final part of the paragraph makes reference to the audience and the way lighting evokes response.

Cheever's function in the scene is to write down John Proctor's confession. He sets up his materials and lights a candle. This is both a symbol of the advancing dawn and a practical way to increase the light as more characters have entered. Spotlights with Deep Straw gels focused on the surrounding area would fade up as the candle is lit. The glow from this light will catch the faces of the key characters so that facial expressions are visible to the audience.

> The second paragraph makes three points about the candle and details its function in the scene. There is further analysis of how the candle symbolises a theme in the extract.

The lighting is significant in this scene because it indicates the passage of time: John Proctor is to hang when the sun rises. The lighting would be programmed to slowly cross-fade from the blue moonlight to a golden dawn, with Gallo Gold gel and a gobo of the jail bars. This light would be positioned at a low angle to recreate the rising sun. By the time Parris says 'The sun is up' a russet light is streaming through the high windows but from a different direction. This is a visual trigger for the pace of the action: there is urgency for Proctor to sign or be hanged. The lighting would be a signal to the audience who will see the sunlight before Parris' line.

> The final paragraph analyses the significance of lighting in the scene and discusses the transition from night to dawn using specific technical terminology. The paragraph ends with a further link to the way lighting affects the audience.

## Overall commentary

This is a strong response because:

- there is a sound knowledge and understanding of the role of the lighting designer
- it relates the design ideas to both the text and the audience
- it has confident and accurate use of subject-specific and technical terminology.

## Overview of Section B

Watching live theatre is exciting and entertaining. You can use everything you have learned to critically analyse and evaluate your live theatre experience. You will also learn skills and collect ideas from experienced theatre-makers that you can use in your practical work. This part of the exam will ask you to analyse and evaluate a performance through two questions. This section is worth 15 marks.

**Top tip**

Take every opportunity you have to see live theatre. Get used to being an informed audience member. Being able to take in as much detail as possible from a live theatre experience will only come with practice.

**Exam tip**

Accessing digital recordings of theatre on the internet or at the cinema will support your understanding of productions. Remember, though: only a live theatre production, where you are in the same space as the performers, can be used in the exam.

**Taking it further**

Go further than offering simple opinions. Show you understand why the elements of the production and performance were selected to communicate meaning. Then decide whether these different elements successfully communicated the meaning.

## Choosing a performance

Theatre can be accessed in many ways in the 21st century. Your teacher will to ensure you experience a live theatre performance that is appropriate for this exam. Here is the guidance that your teacher must use in selecting a production.

- Live theatre means being in the same performance space as the performers. You **cannot** use filmed versions of a stage production in the exam.
- The performance **must not** be sung through in its entirety.
- The performance can be amateur (including the work of peers in your school) or professional, as long as it gives you enough material to meet the demands of the question.
- The performance **must not** be one of the texts from Component 3.

The most important thing is to see a production that will give you lots to write about. Choose to write about a performance that covers a range of production elements: costume, set, lighting, sound and so on as you could be asked to write about any of these.

## Being an informed audience member

The exam requires you to analyse and evaluate a live theatre performance. You will need to use all your knowledge and understanding from this course. There are several exam tips and questions to help you on your way.

It is important to get the most out of each live theatre experience. Here are some suggestions to help you prepare.

- If there is one, you might like to read the play text before you see the performance.
- Write notes during the interval and at the end of the performance while your memory is fresh.
- Use any resources available, to remind you of the performance – for example, the company/production website, its Facebook page, the published programme or resources online.
- If you watched a peer performance in school, talk to the performers and their teacher afterwards.

## Question types

In your exam, you will write about one live theatre experience. You will be able to take 500 words of notes into the exam. Knowing the types of questions you will be asked will help you to gather appropriate notes.

Section B will have **two** questions – both short essay-style questions.

Question (a) will be worth **6 marks**.

Question (b) will be worth **9 marks**.

The questions will ask you to **analyse** and/or **evaluate** specific elements of the production you have seen.

Here is an example of what an analyse question might look like and what it is asking you.

> ### Exam-style question
>
> Analyse how stage space was used to engage the audience during the opening moments of the performance. **(6 marks)**

In this analyse question, you are being asked to look at the stage space in the opening moments of the play. The details you might write about include:

- proxemics, including touch and bodily contact
- entrances and exits
- movement – stillness, pace, direction, size, flow, weight, control, orientation

You should use these details to show your understanding of how the stage space was used to engage the audience during the opening moments of the performance. You could discuss:

- your first impressions of characters
- your first impressions of relationships between characters
- the visual impact of the performers in space to communicate the key themes.

Here is an example of what an evaluate question might look like and what it is asking you.

> ### Exam-style question
>
> Evaluate how colour was used in the lighting of the performance to create impact for the audience. **(9 marks)**

The word 'evaluate' is asking you to offer your opinion on how effective a certain aspect of the performance was. Your opinions must be fully justified with examples from the production.

In this evaluate question you would need to focus on moments where colour was used in the lighting of the performance. This could include how it was used to:

- create mood
- focus attention on an area of the stage space
- focus attention on a character
- focus attention on a relationship
- indicate a change of location or time.

You will need to write about how effective these aspects were. You could do this through:

- a comparison between two moments of colour in lighting that had differing impact on the audience – for example, one positive and one negative
- one overall value judgement (positive or negative) about the impact of colour in lighting at several different moments, with different examples
- a balanced set of examples, some negative and some positive.

# Elements of a production

In your exam there will be different elements of each production that you may need to write about. The following pages look at how you can write extended notes on these elements.

Making notes during your live theatre experience will give you a large set of descriptions that need organising. After your live experience, you should write up your notes neatly and organise your thoughts as soon as possible. These will end up being the 500 words you take into your exam, so make sure they:

- are detailed and extensive
- include some of your initial analysis and evaluation.

Look at the student notes throughout this section (they begin on page 98), which are examples of the kinds of notes you should collect. They are based on the Regent's Park Theatre's production of *Lord of the Flies* at G Live, Guildford.

## The director's vision

In your exam responses, it is important to show an understanding of the director's vision. The director's interpretation of a text and their overall concept is how they want the audience to experience the production. You will have to use your own experience of developing practical work to be able to work out another director's interpretation or concept. To help, there are several examples of the choices made by Marianne Elliot, the director of the National Theatre's performance of *The Curious Incident of the Dog in the Night-Time*.

### The big ideas

A director's concept will focus on some big, central ideas. These are the elements of a production that stand out above all others.

For example, the big ideas of the National Theatre's *The Curious Incident of the Dog in the Night-Time* are the use of:

- a digital, projected set, and
- **physical theatre**.

Both these ideas are central to the director's concept and the interpretation of the novel for the stage.

### Audience's role

The exciting thing about live theatre is that audience members take a role in the production. This could be:

- a very active role where they are moving with the performers in the space – as with **promenade and immersive theatre**
- as a passive observer, watching a tragedy unfold or a comic plot unravel.

## Taking it further

Search newspapers and performance programmes for interviews with the director and information about the director's approach. These will give you insight into their ideas.

## Exam tip

In the performance you see, identify what elements of this production make it different and original. Understanding these elements and the vocabulary related to them will help you in your exam.

## Glossary

**Physical theatre**: A style of theatre performance. This is covered more fully in the vocabulary box on pages 99–100, later in this section.

**Promenade and immersive theatre**: Styles of theatre performance. These are covered more fully in the vocabulary box on page 104, later in this section.

Either way, the director will have considered how the production will engage the audience.

For example, in the National Theatre's *The Curious Incident of the Dog in the Night-Time*, the audience's role is as an observer of the mind of someone with autism. The use of the projected set immerses the audience in the thought processes of the autistic teenager.

### The world of the play

Every director works with designers to create a world of the play that supports the key themes. This world will help to communicate the contents of the plot without relying on the dialogue of the characters.

The director will aim to create a particular atmosphere that keeps the audience engaged and interested.

For example, the team behind the National Theatre's *The Curious Incident of the Dog in the Night-Time* used the versatility of a digitally projected set and physical theatre to communicate the scary and extraordinary world of a teenager with autism.

### Director's intentions

An understanding of the director's intentions will help you to analyse and evaluate the production in your written exam. Identifying the big ideas, the audience's role and the world of the play will help you to recognise the director's intentions. You can use this information to write the intentions as a sentence.

> ### Exam tip
>
> Look for interviews with the director in which they may state their intentions for the production. If you find any, you can quote their words in your exam essays.

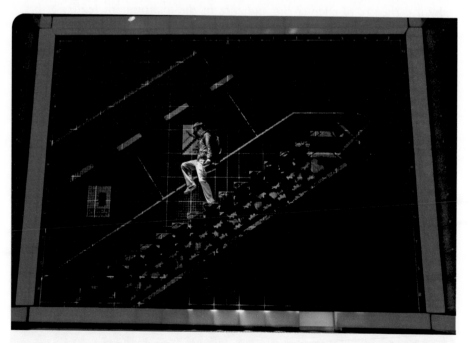

The audience's role in the National Theatre's production of *The Curious Incident of the Dog in the Night-Time*. The audience becomes the observer of the mind of someone with autism.

For example, the director's intentions for the National Theatre's *The Curious Incident of the Dog in the Night-Time* may look something like the text below.

> The director, Marianne Elliott, used a projected set and physical theatre to immerse the audience in the scary and extraordinary world of a teenager with autism.

- Use the name of the director.
- Identify the elements of the production that are the big ideas.
- Use a verb that sums up what the style did to the audience.
- Briefly summarise the world of the play and the content of the plot.

This sentence structure is a good way to start an evaluation, as you can refer to the production's success or failure based on the intentions of the director.

Here are some student notes about the director's intention in a live theatre production of *Lord of the Flies*.

**Student notes**

Notes on Regent's Park Theatre's production of Lord of the Flies at G Live, Guildford

**Director's intention**
The director, Timothy Sheader, used a large scale, naturalistic set and physical theatre to engross the audience in the nightmarish reality of boys stranded on an idyllic island.

The whole set in *Lord of the Flies* (Regent's Theatre Touring Production).

# Style of performance

The identification of distinct styles is only two centuries old. Before that, productions were mostly classified as either tragedy or comedy. Elements from the tragedies and comedies of the Ancient Greeks and Shakespeare can be seen in many different styles. This is because these writers had a huge influence on the directors of the late 19th century and beyond.

Identifying the style of the performance you have seen is important for successful analysis and evaluation. Knowing the style will allow you to recognise particular conventions.

In the following text are:

- a glossary of performance styles
- some student notes on styles.

This information will help you to understand at a deeper level the live performance you will watch. It will also help you to gather notes and write essays about performance styles.

## Vocabulary of performance styles

**Mask**: Physical action and character are reinforced by masks as the main form of communication.

**Naturalism**: The performance is realistic with a focus on human behaviour and psychology. Characters' motivations and actions are rooted in their environment. Conflicts are significant and life-changing, but are presented with everyday speech and movement.

**Realism**: This is similar to naturalism, except characters' actions and motivations are rooted in individual choice rather than environment.

**Expressionism**: The set, props, costume, lighting and sound are created as if they are the imagination of a single character. These elements can often be distorted and dreamlike. The moods created and ideas presented can be more important than the plot. Movement and voice are heightened, with an emphasis on chorus and ensemble.

**Symbolism**: The actions, movements and voice are metaphorical and represent a deeper meaning. Mood and atmosphere link images and ideas that may otherwise lack a precise meaning.

**Epic theatre**: The production guides the audience from identification with characters and themes to a feeling of detachment. This is known as *verfremdungseffekt* or V-Effect. It can be achieved by:

- performers coming out of role
- third-person narration
- the use of placards
- several performers playing the same character
- singing and dancing.

This style makes you think, debate and discuss the themes and issues raised long after the performance has finished. This can be achieved by:

## Exam tips

- If you are asked to analyse a particular element of the production, you can mention conventions of the performance's style within your answer.
- A performance style can help you to make judgements about the success of a production. Evaluating an element of the production (for example, lighting or costume) with reference to the style will make your response stand out for the examiner.

## Activity ?

Some modern productions can be a mixture of styles. List some different mixtures, then discuss what effects these may have on an audience.

# Section B Live theatre evaluation

## Exam tip

Try answering these questions, which will help to guide your analysis and evaluation of performance style in the live performance you have seen.

- How did the style of performance support the big ideas of the production?
- How did the style of performance reinforce the main characters?
- How did specific elements of the style impact on you and the audience?
- Why is the style appropriate for the content of the performance?
- Why does the style support the communication of the director's intentions?

- minimal use of props, costume and set
- a sense of 'fun' that jars with the audience after the performance (known as *spass*)
- combining every element of the performance to communicate an overall political, social or moral essence (known as *gestus*).

**Forum theatre (Theatre of the Oppressed):** The performance challenges different forms of oppression in society by presenting a problem, which is later solved. Sometimes, the audience (spectators, or even 'spect-actors') are invited to give solutions and act them out.

**Theatre of Cruelty:** The production is **not** literally cruel in terms of bloodshed or pain. It is cruel because it aims to challenge and shock the audience and place them at the centre of the drama. This is not like traditional theatre performances.

**Site-specific theatre:** The performance is a direct response to the space. The performance space is an important 'character'.

**Immersive theatre:** There is no fixed order of events for the audience. The performance is a collection of small experiences and interactions for the audience. This interaction makes the audience a 'character' in the play. Meaning and narrative are not fixed. They are created by each individual audience member's experience.

**Verbatim theatre:** All the words used in the production are taken from real life.

**Physical theatre:** Dance and mime, physicality and movement are used to highlight more realistic aspects of a production.

## Student notes

*Notes on Regent's Park Theatre's production of Lord of the Flies at G Live, Guildford*

*Styles*
*Naturalism — Production naturalistic to start with. Realistic set. Focus on boys' behaviour/psychology. Themes — life-changing events, but spoken in slang. Language is recognisable/modern.*

*Expressionism — Set, sound, lighting - all become more distorted as you get further into production. They match boys' evil acts. Production then gets more stylised. Whole cast moves slowly - slow motion. This emphasises key moments — e.g. murders.*

*Physical Theatre — Tribal dances and hunts - all very choreographed. Movements/physical actions - highly planned for effect.*

*Overall thoughts*
*Naturalism shifts to expressionism. Reinforces idea that audience is part of realistic nightmare! Physical theatre used to create ensemble movement — supports idea that boys are becoming a tribe and losing own identities.*

# Set design

A set design is hugely influenced by the style of the performance.

- A naturalistic or realistic set will be truthful to the detail of the location and period. This set will usually have the feeling of a wall (the fourth wall) being removed, leaving the audience looking in on the 'real' lives of the characters.

- An expressionistic set will have obscure angles and be more dreamlike.

In the following text are:

- a glossary of words related to set design
- some student notes.

This information will help you to understand at a deeper level the live performance you will watch. It will also help you to gather notes and write essays about set design.

## Vocabulary of set design

**Period**: The time in history when the play is set. Elements of the production will reinforce the social, historical, cultural and political context of the play.

**Colour**: This works alongside lighting to reinforce mood and atmosphere. The colour of the set will also communicate meaning, especially when it contrasts with the colour of costume or lighting.

**Texture**: This can be used to support the key themes and ideas of a production. For example, a metallic texture will have a very different meaning from earthy textures.

**Entrances and exits**: The position of entrances and exits, and how characters use them, can be significant. This is particularly true of historical productions where they can have symbolic meanings. For example, the trapdoor at the Globe Theatre symbolises 'hell'. Modern productions still draw on these traditions: powerful characters enter from *upstage centre* or from a raised part of the stage.

**Set changes**: These can take place alongside changes in the play and can give the audience clues about things like time, era or general mood.

**Projection**: This can be used to create a set, or show film or images. The amount of projection can impact the style of a performance.

- It can have the distancing effect (*verfremdungseffekt* or V-Effect) of epic theatre.

- It can also create dreamlike worlds of the Expressionist style.

- The audience should be able to identify the world created in the projection and how this differs from the rest of the play.

## Taking it further

Think about textures that:

- are associated with a city
- are associated with the countryside
- communicate the future or the past
- cover the floor of a set.

When you are next in a live performance (or even watching a performance onscreen) note down how texture can reinforce the story of the play, while perhaps symbolising broader themes.

## Top tip

Make sure you note all set changes in detail at your live theatre experience. Understanding these changes and the vocabulary associated with them will help in your exam.

- Be aware of how one set can contrast a previous set.
- Note whether the set feels more open or closed and claustrophobic.
- Note also whether one main set is changed to show, for example, time passing or to represent the character's mindset.

## Activity

1   Draw and label a stage map using upstage, downstage, stage left, stage right and any other stage areas you know.
2   Note down what you think the different entrance and exit points mean.
3   Experiment with these points in your drama studio while improvising basic mimed scenes.

## Taking it further

Research the social, historical, cultural and political context:

- Read the introduction to the play text.
- Ask a history teacher about the period and look at relevant history textbooks to give you a sense of the period.
- Ask your art and music teachers about popular culture at the time the play was set.

## Exam tip

Try answering these questions, which will help to guide your analysis and evaluation of set design in the live performance you have seen.

- Why did the set communicate the world of the play?
- How did the set link to the characters' thoughts and feelings?
- How did the set make you feel as a member of the audience? Are these feelings similar to a character's feelings? Why?
- Why were the position of the entrances and exits significant?
- How did the set provide obstacles for the characters? What did this mean?

Here are some student notes about set design in a live theatre production of *Lord of the Flies*.

## Student notes

Notes on Regent's Park Theatre's production of Lord of the Flies at G Live, Guildford

### Style of performance
Crash site – naturalistic. Has section of full-size fuselage!! Set has moving parts – falling walls of fuselage/cracks in wing. Supports expressionistic nightmare plot.

### Colour and texture
Natural colours/textures of sand/jungle all mixed up with man-made fabrics and metals. Man-made stuff/metal shows what was in the plane when it crashed. Man-made stuff moved around a lot. Actors use it more than natural stuff.

### Entrances and exits
Entrances and exits – five main ones.
- downstage right – no obstacles
- downstage left – mound of luggage to climb over
- upstage left, higher level – onto tail wing
- top of stage, right wing – medium level
- upstage centre – behind jungle and plane.

### Set changes
Set stayed same but had things added during interval. Pre-set on show from when we sat down. Changes made in full view by stage hands. You could see them do it. Fuselage wall fell down and cracks opened in plane wing – these must have been mechanical changes.

### Overall thoughts
Set – like a monstrous character in its own right! Seemed to come alive as boys got more evil. Set really interested me – realistic island, which fell apart. Gave a sense of terror. Entrances and exits used to explain character status – the different characters used different entrances/exits.

## Use of the stage space

Stage space questions require you to make connections between performance and space. You will always need to write about how the actors use the space.

- The pace of movement and the distance between actors (proxemics) can hold meaning for the audience.

- The interaction of the performer and space can have symbolic meaning, especially in historical theatre. Performers interact with the space in terms of height, depth and width. Where the performer is positioned in the space can communicate status. You must consider how their position communicates status in relation to other characters and in relation to the audience.

### Top tip

In your live performance evaluation, look out for where in the space particular moments take place. Note whether these places in the space have a symbolic meaning. Understanding this and the related vocabulary will help in your exam.

# Section B Live theatre evaluation

## Glossary

**Fourth wall**: The notion that the stage is like a room with four walls, with the audience looking in where one of the walls would be.

## Activity ?

Try out all the audience configurations that are possible in your drama studio.

1   Place seats in the configurations and try acting scenes from any of your work.
2   Note how you have to act differently in the different configurations.
3   Note whether the impact on the audience changes.

## Exam tip

Try answering these questions, which will help to guide your analysis and evaluation on stage space in the live performance you have seen.

- How did the stage space link to the characters' thoughts and feelings (for example, trapped)?
- How did the stage space support the set design?
- How did the stage space support the style of the performance?
- How did the director maximise the stage space?
- Why were the audience put in this configuration? Did you feel connected to the characters or distant? Why?

The stage space and the style of performance have strong connections.

- Naturalistic theatre traditionally takes place in a proscenium arch space, as the proscenium acts like a **fourth wall** on the world of the play.
- Other styles of theatre use spaces that allow them to break down the divide between audience and performance.

There are many different types of stage spaces, from small studio spaces to huge amphitheatres. Most professional productions will have chosen their space carefully so that it fully supports the performance. Some theatres are flexible spaces and can adapt their seating arrangements for the audience.

In the following text are:

- a glossary of words related to the use of stage space
- some student notes on stage space.

This information will help you to understand at a deeper level the live performance you will watch. It will also help you to gather notes and write essays about stage space.

## Vocabulary of stage space

**End-on-stage**: This is often found in a studio theatre where the seats face the stage space at one end. There is no proscenium arch.

**Promenade and Immersive**: These can be found spaces or non-theatre spaces. Audience members walk through the space to experience the performance.

**Site-specific theatre**: These spaces are chosen as a key part of the production. The performance links directly to the space that it is performed in.

**Traverse**: The audience are positioned on two sides of the space with the performance taking place in the middle.

**In-the-round**: The audience are seated all the way around the performance space.

**Thrust**: The performance space thrusts out into the audience. The audience sit or stand on three sides of the stage space.

**Proscenium arch**: The audience sit facing a stage at one end. The stage is framed with a proscenium arch. More and more traditional proscenium arch spaces are adding small thrusts to break the divide between the audience and the performance space.

**Amphitheatre**: The audience sit in a large and steep half-bowl shape with a circular stage at the bottom. The Olivier Theatre at the National Theatre is designed as an amphitheatre.

Here are some student notes about stage space in a live theatre production of *Lord of the Flies*.

---

### Student notes

*Notes on Regent's Park Theatre's production of Lord of the Flies at G Live, Guildford*

*Types of stage space*
*Proscenium arch – Kind of thrust where sand and luggage came into auditorium space. Boys would lie on it or be pushed down it. It was very steep! You felt part of the action, because the thrust was close. But separate because of proscenium arch.*

*Height, depth and width – Different heights showed status of tribes and individuals. You could see how important/not important they were. Very useful to see the contrasts.*

*Overall thoughts*
*Stage space – VERY important! Used to show territories. So much on it, including crashed plane. Made you feel trapped – closed in. Meant you could see how Jack, Ralph and Roger used their power – proxemics! Great for the audience – drawn in all the time. Felt like you were watching a film.*

---

### Glossary

**Auditorium**: The part of the theatre in which the audience sits. It is also known as the house.

---

## Lighting design

The lighting designer's role is to create clarity of meaning through lighting choices. To create meaning they can use:

- different colours and patterns
- brightness
- focus
- different kinds of lights.

Naturalistic and realistic performances will use lighting that supports the everyday feel of the production. There may be subtle shifts in location or time of day that have meaning in these styles. All other styles will use lighting to guide the audience's eye and imagination.

In the following text are:

- a glossary of words related to lighting design
- some student notes on lighting design.

This information will help you to understand at a deeper level the live performance you will watch. It will also help you to gather notes and write essays about lighting design.

# Section B Live theatre evaluation

Top tip

## Top tip

Lighting decisions can give clues about the text. Familiarise yourself with the vocabulary about lighting. Know what to look for and make notes for your exam. Check to see which part of the stage is more brightly lit. Try to work out why.

- Check the lighting in different scenes and note how it has changed. Note also whether this change contrasts with or supports the narrative.
- Identify different colours of lights. Decide what those colours mean in relation to the play at that point.
- Identify whether the lighting creates a positive or negative tone.
- Identify patterns and shapes of lighting, and the mood and atmosphere they create. Note how they relate to colour and intensity of the lighting.

## Activity ?

Test the different lighting possibilities in a dark room.

1 Use a lantern with a handle or a torch with a strong beam. Point it at a person or object.

2 Now change the position of the lantern or torch. Note down the mood created by the different angles.

3 Hold coloured gels over your light source. Note the different meanings you can create through these colours.

## Vocabulary of lighting design

**Focus**: Lighting is used to draw the audience's attention to particular parts of the performance. Characters, set or props can be picked out precisely. The lighting design can give emphasis to important moments in the performance.

**Intensity**: This is how bright the audience perceives the light to be. The lighting designer uses a mixture of intensity to create particular effects.

**Colour, mood and atmosphere**: Colour is created using gels that sit in front of the light source. Modern lighting also uses LED technology to be able to shift more economically from one light colour to the next. The colours of lighting and their intensity can create mood and atmosphere for a scene.

**Pattern and shape**: Plates or screens, called gobos, can be placed in front of a source of a light to create patterns. Barn doors on the edges of a light fitting and the shutter size in the light fixture can create different shapes. The edge-quality of these shapes can be hard or soft.

**Position and direction**: This can have a big impact on the subject being lit. They can be:

- frontlit
- backlit
- lit from a high angle
- lit from a low angle.

The light can come from either side. The position and direction of light can create shadows that affect mood and atmosphere.

### Types of lighting

Here is a basic selection of lighting (both halogen bulb and LED) that is commonly used.

- **Floodlight**: Lights a large area with no edge. No lens means no focus.
- **PAR can**: Lights large area with an edge. The lens allows for some focus.
- **Fresnel**: Small fixture that gives a soft-edged spot of light. There is little flexibility in the size of focus.
- **Profile spot**: Long fixture that gives a hard-edged spot of light. Very flexible in the size of focus.
- **Moving heads**: Automated lights that offer flexibility and variation.

## Exam tip

You will find it useful to be able to name the kinds of lights that are used in stage lighting. This is the type of subject-specific vocabulary that can be used in an essay to make you stand out from other candidates.

Here are some student notes about lighting in a live theatre production of *Lord of the Flies*.

## Student notes

*Notes on Regent's Park Theatre's production of Lord of the Flies at G Live, Guildford*

*Key lighting moments*

*Red strobe effect – Used on wing tip - rear. Flashed during pre-set and when things got violent!*

*Yellow/green wash – Used in early part as main lighting. This was when the boys were getting on together - exploring and playing games. Leaves – made by gobos. Very gentle in texture.*

*Blue wash – Linked Simon's speech with night-time. Showed contrast between beauty and danger on island.*

*Red/orange wash – Showed gentle glow of fire to start with. Then got stronger – to show violence of a hunt. Light was very intense. Came from back of stage. Made silhouettes of the boys.*

*White spotlight – This followed Piggy – especially when he was hunted by the others. It was very pale against the red wash. When Piggy was murdered the whole stage turned red.*

*Overall thoughts*

*Lighting helped with mood. Greens and yellows were like hope. But red was like danger and violence. Hard to look at the strobe. Felt unpleasant – probably to make us think about unpleasant themes in the play. As the lighting went from lighter to darker, the boys were losing their innocence and things were getting more evil.*

## Exam tip

Try answering these questions, which will help to guide your analysis and evaluation on lighting design in the live performance you have seen.

- How were your emotions triggered by the lighting designer's choices?
- How was the world of the play supported by lighting choices?
- How did the intensity of the lights physically affect your eyes? Why do you think the lighting designer wanted this effect?
- Why did the lights support the big ideas and themes of the performance?
- Why were the contrasts created by the lighting designer significant to the meaning of the play?

A violent scene, lit with a red wash for effect, in *Lord of the Flies* (Regent's Theatre Touring Production).

Understanding sound design and music, and the vocabulary that goes with it, will help you when you do your live performance evaluation. Make sure you can write about:

- the emotional effect of the sound and music on you individually
- whether the music used went against the content of the scene (remind yourself of *verfremdungseffekt* on page 99)
- the exact sound effects used and how they complemented the action
- whether the effects were realistic or distorted
- any songs that were sung
- any shifts in the pitch of music and sound (a high pitch can have a very different effect from a low pitch)
- any changes in volume and their significance in the performance.

Your ability to describe sound in these ways will give you more detail for your analysis and evaluation.

## Activity ?

Find a selection of different mood music online.

1. Try searching 'instrumental nightmare music' or 'instrumental happy music', for example.
2. Improvise a scene of a person leaving home.
3. Repeat this scene several times to different pieces of music.
4. Discuss the effect of the different music on your scene. Note whether the meaning of the scene changed if the music didn't fit.

## Sound design and music

Styles of performance will have particular types of sound and music that you should be able to identify.

- Naturalistic plays will have everyday sound effects with music used during transitions.
- Expressionistic plays will have dreamlike or nightmarish music and sounds that complement the stylised action.

In the following text are:

- a glossary of words related to the use of sound design and music
- some student notes on sound design and music.

This information will help you to understand at a deeper level the live performance you will watch. It will also help you to gather notes and write essays about sound design and music.

## Vocabulary of sound design and music

**Genre of music**: The type of music that features in the production – for example, rock, pop, classical, folk, hip hop, drum'n'bass, etc.

**Mood and atmosphere**: Music and sound have a huge impact on the emotional experience of the audience. The sadness of a scene can be increased with the use of sad music. But the same scene performed with upbeat music can have a very different impact.

**Sound effects**: These punctuate the narrative, action and all aspects of live performance. The effects can literally be any type of sound.

**Live or recorded**: Music and sound can be created live or be pre-recorded and played digitally. Live music can be performed by musicians separate from the acting company or it can be played by the actors themselves. Live music can be amplified through speakers or played without speakers.

**Pitch**: This relates to whether a sound is high or low.

**Volume**: Volume is carefully controlled by the sound designer when developing the play. Sudden high volume can jolt an audience and a sustained loud sound will be uncomfortable for the audience.

**Direction**: Speakers and live musicians can be positioned anywhere within the space. The direction of sounds and music can impact on an audience. Sound effects that appear to come from behind an audience in a proscenium arch theatre immerse the audience in the action.

Here are some student notes about lighting in a live theatre production of *Lord of the Flies*.

## Student notes

*Notes on Regent's Park Theatre's production of Lord of the Flies at G Live, Guildford*

*Recorded music*
*Pre-recorded music — choral, had eerie feel.*

*Mood and atmosphere — When something big happened, the music was used — like hunting or murder. Boys' choir — fitted all the choir characters. For Simon, the normal choral music worked with how he felt about beauty and danger. But the music was also mixed in other ways — loud and distorted during his murder.*

*Direction — Came from speaker. It was behind the jungle/trees, to side of proscenium arch.*

*Overall thoughts*
*Choral music let us know how people felt — it was very tense and awesome! It let us understand what boys were thinking. Beautiful when island was a good place. Horrible/loud when island became like hell. It was the same music — just used in different ways and distorted to show different things. It was very high during hunting and murders. Distorted.*

## Exam tip

Try answering these questions, which will help to guide your analysis and evaluation on sound design and music in the live performance you have seen.

- How did the sound and music affect your emotions? Did these emotions match the emotions of the characters or did they jar? Why?
- How did the sound and music affect you physically? Why?
- How did the sound and music create the world of the play?
- How did sound and music support climaxes?
- Why did the use of live or recorded sound and music support the big ideas of the play?

## Costume

The costume designer plays an important role in creating practical and meaningful designs. The costume in the live performance you see may follow the conventions of a particular style or genre of theatre.

- The costumes of a naturalistic play will be very different from an expressionistic production.
- Physical theatre will have different priorities from those of epic theatre.

Meaning will be communicated through the costume design in many subtle ways. In the following text are:
- a glossary of words related to the use of costume
- some student notes on costume.

This information will help you to understand at a deeper level the live performance you will watch. It will also help you to gather notes and write essays about costume.

## Taking it further

The website of the performance you see may have the designs for the production available for you to look at. Alternatively, you could email the production team to explain that you are studying drama and preparing for an exam, and ask if they can send you some photographs of costume designs.

## Top tip

Understanding costume design, and the vocabulary that goes with it, will help you in your exam. Make sure you:

- produce sketches of what garments are worn by each character
- can identify items of clothing added or removed (and when this happened)
- do some historical and cultural research to understand the significance of different garments and fabrics
- can identify the broader fashions represented in the performance
- can describe a costume's shape and fit – for example, whether it has hard or soft edges, hugs the figure, disguises the body's shape, reveals areas of the body, has been ripped or modified. This will allow you to make points about characters, relationships and themes.

Your ability to describe costume design in these ways will give you more detail for the analysis and evaluation you require in your writing.

## Vocabulary of costume design

**Period**: The costume design will often give a strong indication of time. This will be supported by other elements of the production. The audience will make particular judgements about the content, themes and ideas based on the historical period of the production. Some productions try to be 'timeless' to support themes and ideas. This could mean a mixture of periods has been brought together or there is an emphasis on neutrality. Neutrality can be achieved through simplicity, with the costume designer using colour, material and shape rather than historical features.

**Garments**: Items of clothing can indicate character, status and location.

**Colour**: Colour can communicate broad meaning for audiences. It can trigger subconscious associations that will inform how an audience feels about the content of the production.

**Material**: This communicates meaning to the audience. For example, people often associate fabrics with different levels of wealth and status – especially in some historical or cultural contexts.

**Fit and shape**: These give clues about characters, relationships and themes.

**Hair and make-up**: These link to particular styles. For example, expressionist theatre often uses pale, white faces with black eyes. They can also communicate a character's control at particular points. Hair and make-up are closely linked with cultural ideas of status. Make-up could be used to reinforce an incident or injury.

## Activity

Create a collage of images that capture the clothing of a period (you choose which period).

1. Ask a partner to shut their eyes while you describe the items of clothing. Try to be as detailed as possible.

2. Discuss with your partner how your descriptions made them feel. Encourage them to tell you all their ideas.

### The meaning of colours

Colours are often thought to have different meanings:

- **red** can mean passion, desire, love, war and danger
- **yellow** can mean joy, happiness, cowardice and caution
- **green** can mean growth, harmony, fertility and jealousy
- **blue** can mean depth, trust, truth, depression
- **purple** can mean power, wisdom, luxury, arrogance
- **black** can mean power, elegance, formality, mystery, death and evil
- **white** can mean purity, peace, cold and clinical.

These colours, used in costume design, can all say something about the character and the plot.

Costume for *Lord of the Flies* (Regent's Theatre Touring Production).

Here are some student notes about costume design in a live theatre production of *Lord of the Flies*.

## Student notes

*Notes on Regent's Park Theatre's production of Lord of the Flies at G Live, Guildford*

### Costume and characterisation

Jack/choirboys – started with gowns/mortar boards. Others/Ralph had school jumpers and ties. Some had been spoilt in the crash. Very naturalistic. After a while on the island, they turned their ties into tribal headbands. Their shirts got ripped and were open. Trousers got ripped and made into shorts. We didn't see these costume changes. They happened off stage.

### Colour

Ralph – blue jumper to show depth and trust.

Jack – black gown/jumper to show how formal he was and evil.

Simon – purple jumper. Wisdom.

### Hair and make-up

Hair got more untidy as play went on. Blood from pig made war-paint. This got better designed as play went on.

### Overall thoughts

School uniforms – represented order and formality at start of play.

Gowns – these made Jack and the choir different from other boys. Created a distance. Audience could to relate to Ralph (uniform) better than Jack (choir gown). So they sympathised more with him. As uniforms got worse/ripped, the boys got more violent and tribal.

# Section B Live theatre evaluation

## Acting

The acting style is at the heart of all the styles of performance. All the different styles use design elements to reinforce particular acting styles. Familiarise yourself with the kind of acting that is likely to feature in the production you will see. Remember that 'naturalistic' acting will feature in all the styles but it will be given a twist that will change the audience's response. This twist will be an exaggeration of one or more elements of acting.

In the following text are:

- a glossary of words related to acting style
- some student notes on acting style.

This information will help you to understand at a deeper level the live performance you will watch. It will also help you to gather notes and write essays about the process of acting.

## Vocabulary of acting styles and how they are achieved

### Voice

**Articulation**: Emphasis on consonants or vowels.

**Pitch**: Continuum of high to low quality.

**Pace**: Continuum of fast to slow delivery.

**Pause**: Choice of breaks in speech and their length.

**Tone**: Choice of the mood or emotion of delivery.

**Inflection**: Choice of stress or emphasis.

**Volume**: Continuum of loud to quiet.

### Movement

**Pace**: Continuum of fast to slow.

**Direction**: Up/down, side to side, backwards/forwards.

**Size**: Continuum of big to small.

**Flow**: Continuum of free to restricted.

**Weight**: Continuum of heavy to light.

**Control**: Continuum of stable to unstable.

**Orientation**: Choice of where the body is facing.

### Non-verbal communication

**Spatial behaviour (proxemics)**: Physical distance between characters.

**Facial expression**: Change in the face to communicate emotion.

**Gesture**: Movement of the hands to communicate an idea or give meaning and emphasis.

**Gaze**: Direction that a character is looking, including eye contact.

**Non-verbal vocalisations**: Noise and sounds that do not include language.

**Posture**: The position of the body.

**Touch and bodily contact**: Physical connections between two people.

Here are some student notes about acting in a live theatre production of *Lord of the Flies*.

## Student notes

Notes on Regent's Park Theatre's production of Lord of the Flies at G Live, Guildford

### Style

Acting style – started as naturalistic. Boys were definitely school children. Then it got more stylised as boys became more tribal/dangerous. You could see that the boys started as normal but then mentally fell apart.

### Characters

Ralph (James Phoon) and Piggy (Anthony Roberts) – Ralph spoke posh/properly. Piggy had an accent. Ralph had a deep voice. And he spoke steadily. Piggy was more frenetic and he got high pitched sometimes. Ralph had controlled movements. He seemed strong. Like he knew what he was doing. Piggy slumped. He was negative. He would move away from Ralph if he got too close.

Jack (Freddie Watkins) and choir entrance – Dominated choir boys. He led them in a line. Was a bit like a teacher – loud/bossy. He pointed and showed his fists. Upright. High chin. Looked superior. He was quite thin, but his movements were big and strong. When he was frustrated his voice would get high/shrill. The choir boys were the opposite - slouched, quiet, no confidence.

Roger (Matthew Castle) – Quiet. Sinister – right from the beginning. He didn't look much at the others. When he spoke he was slow, sinister to start with. Then, later, he started to make eye contact, and his speaking got quicker and more erratic to show him becoming blood thirsty with the hunt. He moved like an animal. Like a squatted ape in the plane, then a gorilla later to frighten Piggy during final hunt.

Simon (Keenan Munn-Francis) – Deep thinker. Could see what was really happening on the island. Movements - mainly head and eyes. Slow and with purpose. He showed authority to the audience – on stage he was more towards the audience. Voice – steady pace, delicate tone. But it gets louder and more aggressive when he is possessed by the beastie.

## Activity

Place two people in an empty space. Face away from them as they arrange a non-verbal image. They should start with changing proxemics and gaze. Then they should try changing facial expressions, posture and gestures. Every time you turn around to look at them, try to describe the meaning of the scene they have created.

> ### Exam tip
>
> Try answering these questions, which will help to guide your analysis and evaluation on acting styles in the live performance you have seen.
>
> - How did voice and movement choices support the content and world of the play?
> - How did characters' voices contrast? Why?
> - How did characters' movements contrast? Why?
> - Why did particular vocal and movement choices have an emotional impact on the audience?
> - How did non-verbal communication contrast what was being said by characters? Why was this subtext important?

The tribal/animalistic boys hunting in *Lord of the Flies* (Regent's Theatre Touring Production).

Here are some student notes about acting in a live theatre production of *Lord of the Flies*.

---

**Student notes**

*Notes on Regent's Park Theatre's production of Lord of the Flies at G Live, Guildford*

*Hunting and murder*
*Movement – animalistic and ritualistic. Had a pattern but not regular. Chaotic. Feet stamped – fists clenched – hands above head. Choral speaking – like a chant, joyous but aggressive.*

*Overall thoughts*
*Acting choices – clear contrast, reinforces conflict and aggression. Audience can relate to voice and movement of Ralph – not Jack. Animal-like movements dominate space – getting more powerful. Civilised beginning – naturalistic. Violent end – stylised/animalistic.*

---

## Impact on the audience

You must be aware of the way in which all the different elements of a production impact on:

- you as an individual
- the audience as a whole.

Remember that a production can have a physical impact as well as an emotional one. It may be rare, but you should be able to describe, for example, how an element of the production made your heartbeat race.

Knowing how a production made **you** feel is one thing. Generalising for the whole audience is quite another and can sometimes be tricky. However, it is possible to:

- sense the feeling of a group or audience
- observe physical responses from the rest of the audience.

All of these levels of awareness can complement the analysis and evaluations in your essays.

---

**Top tip**

Research reviews of the production in newspapers and online. This will help to gauge the sense of audience response.

---

**Top tip**

Writing clear and precise descriptions of the way elements of the production made you feel will give you lots of opportunity for analysis and evaluation. Make sure that any discussion of impact is fully justified by clear examples of elements of the production.

---

**Exam tip**

Writing clear and precise descriptions of the way elements of the production made you feel will give you lots of opportunity for analysis and evaluation. Make sure that any discussion of impact is fully justified by clear examples of elements of the production.

# Section B: Live theatre evaluation

**Question 9 (a)**

*Analyse how stage space was used to engage the audience during the opening moments of the performance.* **(6 marks)**

These are sections of students' responses to show the different levels of response.

. . . . . . . . . . . . . . . . . . . . . . . . . . . . . . . . . . . . . . . . . . . . . . . . . . . . . . . . . . . . . . . . . . . . . . . .

## Student A

James Phoon (Ralph) entered the set at the start of the play looking around with his mouth open in awe at the island. I could tell that Ralph was a confident character because Phoon's movements seemed to flow and glide across the debris. Anthony Roberts (Piggy) chose to stumble and trip over the debris when he joined Phoon on stage. The different ways they moved through the space showed me that Ralph was more powerful than Piggy.

> The first paragraph is clearly structured to include a relevant point about a character's use of space, then this is followed by a specific and detailed example of something that happened on stage. The final sentence refers to the personal experience of the student.

The actor's position in the space supported the idea that Ralph was the higher status. Phoon stood still and upright in the centre of the space as he spoke to Piggy. Roberts (Piggy) had a slouched posture and didn't stop moving. Phoon controlled the centre of the stage space and this meant he was the audience's main focus.

> This student sticks to the question, and writes clearly about stage space rather than drifting off to mention a different production element.

Freddie Watkins (Jack) used levels at the start of the play to show his status by entering from the stage right at the top of the broken wing. I could tell that Jack was more strict than Ralph because Watkins chose to move through the space confidently marching with straight arms. Watkins' entrance and use of space showed that he also had high status but in a different way to Phoon (Ralph).

> The specific examples are really helpful and show an obvious understanding of how actors communicate with their audience.

Watkins also used his position in the space to communicate Jack's authority. He stood upright at the front of a line of boys making sure they didn't move out of line. His position at the front of the line communicated to the audience that Jack wanted to be the most powerful character.

> The rest of the answer includes even more drama vocabulary and specific examples from the production, so it is easy to picture what they saw on stage. Finally, this student is able to link everything they have seen on stage through the wider themes of the play, in this case, power and authority.

. . . . . . . . . . . . . . . . . . . . . . . . . . . . . . . . . . . . . . . . . . . . . . . . . . . . . . . . . . . . . . . . . . . . . . . .

## Overall commentary

This is a strong response because:

- it is a balanced and thorough response
- examples use subject-specific terminology to communicate their full engagement and analysis
- the whole response has interconnected points that show a complete analysis.

. . . . . . . . . . . . . . . . . . . . . . . . . . . . . . . . . . . . . . . . . . . . . . . . . . . . . . . . . . . . . . . . . . . . . . . .

## Student B

*James Phoon (Ralph) and Anthony Roberts (Piggy) use proxemics and levels to communicate their relationship at the start of the play. Phoon moves up close to Roberts when they first meet. Roberts moves away from him and sits on the floor. Phoon doesn't give up and uses close proxemics again and stands over Roberts. The close proxemics and high level shows the audience that Phoon commands the space.*

*Freddie Watkins (Jack) controls how the other actors stand in the space to communicate that his character is a control freak. Watkins arranges the actors playing the choir boys in a line and marches them across the space. When the others move out of line Watkins uses close proxemics to make them return to order. Watkins' ability to control a group by moving closer to them in the space communicates to the audience that he is playing a powerful character.*

This answer is also well structured and makes good points about proxemics and levels. The specific and detailed example about Piggy's movements is really helpful. The final part of the paragraph links directly to the question that was asked. The student specifically says how the use of space communicated power to the audience.

The second paragraph also contains good drama vocabulary. The example of Watkins' control in the space is specific and shows how space can be used to show order. The student clearly communicates the effect of the use of space on the audience.

## Overall commentary

This is an average response because:

- it is a balanced response that answers the question
- examples use appropriate subject-specific terminology to support analysis
- the whole response is presented as separate points.

## Student C

*Ralph explores the island after he has survived a plane crash. He bumps into Piggy and they talk about how amazing the island is. Ralph asks him about his name and laughs at him. Ralph can do handstands and shows Piggy how to do it. I liked Ralph because he was confident. Ralph tries to get Piggy to be more interesting by getting close to him and speaking with an enthusiastic voice. Jack is marching around the island with the choir until they arrive at the crash site where Ralph and Piggy are. Jack is very posh and speaks with a high-pitched voice. I feel sorry for the choir boys as they have to stand still and quiet in a line. Jack acts like their teacher and stands out because he doesn't stand in a line.*

Unfortunately, this response tells us more about the plot of the play rather than concentrating on the use of stage space in performance. It would be better to use the names of the actors to analyse what they did on stage rather than drift into explaining how the characters feel about each other.

## Overall commentary

This is a weak response because

- it reports the narrative rather than presenting examples of performance
- examples aren't relevant to the question and lack subject-specific language
- the whole response lacks clarity and analysis.

# Section B : Live Theatre Evaluation

**Question 9 (a)**

*Analyse how the voice was used to engage the audience during one key moment of the performance.*

These are sections of students' responses to show the different levels of response.

**(6 marks)**

## Student A

James Phoon (Ralph) used a calm and reassuring tone as he guided Anthony Roberts (Piggy) across the stage during the final hunt scene. Phoon had a loud volume and slow pace that was strong and clear for the characters he guided. Phoon's voice pulled me into the scene and made me feel comfortable and confident that they would make it to safety.

The first sentence of this answer tells us that the student is focusing on the question asked. They follow this with a detailed and specific example to support their point. This makes sense to the reader and it is easy to picture even for someone who hasn't seen the same production.

The action is then cross-cut and Phoon's scene freezes whilst Freddie Watkins (Jack) scene begins to move. Watkins speaks with a loud volume and high pitched voice immediately getting the audience to shift their attention. His tone of voice was aggressive towards his group and made me feel nervous about what they might do. The actors' contrasting vocal choices made it clear for the audience that the hunt scene would not end well.

The second paragraph is also very good because it makes a clear and relevant point about the contrasting voices of Jack and Ralph. This is followed by specific and detailed example of how the actors used their voices.

As the two groups got closer to meeting, another important contrast was the rhythm of Phoon and Watkins' voices. Phoon (Ralph) used a steady and natural rhythm of voice that showed me that he was trying to keep his group calm and stay in control. Watkins' (Jack) voice was not natural and sounded more like a chant showing me that his character had become a savage. The contrasting choice of rhythm in the actor's voice during the cross-cut scenes clashed for the audience. This clash of voices communicated that there would be a violent clash between the groups at the end.

The third paragraph uses even more drama vocabulary to make a point about rhythm and climax. This shows that the student understands the role of this scene in relation to the whole play. Again, the analysis focuses on how the contrasting voices create meaning and atmosphere for the audience which links back nicely to the question asked.

## Overall commentary

This is a strong response because:

- it is a balanced and thorough response
- examples use subject-specific terminology to communicate their full engagement and analysis
- the whole response has interconnected points that show a thorough analysis.

# Preparing for your exam

## Student B

James Phoon (Ralph) used a calm tone of voice when he is trying to get his group to safety at the end of the play. He speaks with a slow pace and low pitch as he tries to stop the group being scared. Phoon's choice of voice made the audience feel calm and safe as well.

Freddie Watkins (Jack) used an aggressive tone of voice when he is trying to get his group to hunt Ralph's group at the end. He speaks with a fast pace and a high pitch as he tries push his group forward. Watkins' choice of voice was horrible to listen to and intimidated the audience.

Anthony Roberts (Piggy) used a forceful tone when he is trying to stop the groups fighting at the end. He speaks with a soft volume and a fast pace as he tries to stop the violence. Roberts' choice of voice was almost drowned out by the violence and showed the audience that there was no hope.

> The answer is well structured and uses lots of drama vocabulary, but the paragraphs lacks the confidence of a top answer because the points aren't linked together.

> The student does make use of some specific examples but does not develop these to include an awareness of the effect these vocal performances had on the audience.

> The final sentence makes a helpful connection with the wider themes of the play which shows an understanding of how meaning was created.

## Overall commentary

This is an average response because:

- it is a balanced response that answers the question
- examples use appropriate subject-specific terminology to support analysis
- the full engagement of the student is not fully communicated in the whole response.

## Student C

All the characters projected their voices well throughout the production but one moment that was particularly engaging for me as an audience member was the moment the two tribes clashed and Ralph and Jack spoke really well because I could tell what their characters were thinking by what they said to their friends, for example, Ralph was calm with his group and told them to 'All form a line' he said this softly but I could still hear him because he projected his voice but Jack was aggressive and harsh when he spoke to his group it was like he was possessed, none of his words were lost though as he spoke clearly enough I particularly liked the line 'You've got to have respect for the chief' It really stood out for me as he was clearly stronger than the other boys his gestures were also strong to make his group listen he would point and shake his fist aggressively I think this meant that he was better than Ralph because he was doing more acting.

> The student only refers to the basic idea of projection in relation to voice. To gain higher marks they must give more specific examples by using more complex subject-specific terminology such as pitch, pace, tone and volume.

> The quotations are helpful but it does not refer to how meaning was created with voice and focuses on clarity of volume instead.

> Finally, the student mentions gesture and movement but this would not gain any marks because it doesn't relate to the question.

## Overall commentary

This is a weak response because:

- it reports the lines spoken rather than presenting examples of performance
- there is a lack of engagement with the meaning created by the actors' vocal choices
- the whole response lacks clarity and analysis.

# Section B : Live Theatre Evaluation

**Question 9 (b)**

*Evaluate how colour was used in the lighting of the performance to create impact for the audience.* **(9 marks)**

These are sections of students' responses to show the different levels of response.

## Student A

The pre-set of the Lord of the Flies had a crashed plane with a red flashing light on the tip of the tail wing. The red light flashed with a strobe effect and immediately communicated danger to the audience. As I looked over the impressive set my eyes kept looking at the red flash. The flashing red light returned at all the most violent bits of the play getting faster and faster. It definitely supported the violent action and created impact for the audience because it was uncomfortable to look at.

> This is a strong opening to the evaluation with a clear appreciation of how the pre-set impacted the audience. The student makes a clear connection between the red flashing light and violence. The evaluation is fully justified by the reference to the way the audience was made to feel uncomfortable.

A yellow/green wash was used to set the scene of a beautiful island for the audience. It was used in the early scenes of the boys having fun playing rugby with the conch and going for an adventure. The colour communicated happy sunlight to the audience. This was supported by the high angle of the lights and the gobo of leaves. The yellow/green colour was calm and had a positive impact on the audience. It supported the idea that the boys were innocent at the start.

> There is a high level of detail in the second paragraph as the student uses subject specific terminology to make their analysis clear. There is an understanding of how position and shape of light can communicate meaning to the audience.

A pale, white light was used to light Anthony Roberts (Piggy) and represented his purity. This light stood out the most when Piggy is hunted by the other boys. He is standing on the top of the plane lit with white whilst the other boys are on the lower level lit with red. This contrast of colours had visual impact for the audience and showed them Piggy was pure but in a lot of danger. When Piggy is pushed off the back of the plane to his death there is no white light left. The stage is just filled with a red wash that shows the audience that violence has taken over the island completely.

> The choice of analysis in the final paragraph makes a clear connection with the ideas in the two other paragraphs. This awareness of the use of lighting in the whole production leads to sophisticated evaluations.

## Overall commentary

This is a strong response because:

- the examples are chosen wisely and allow the student to offer a thorough evaluation
- conclusions are personal and fully justified
- the detail of the response and the strong use of technical language demonstrates the student's full engagement with the production.

## Student B

A green light was used to support the setting of a jungle island. It was used at the start of the play when the boys first met and explored the island. The use of a green gel clearly communicated the jungle setting to the audience.

A blue light was used to show the audience that it was night-time on the island. The blue light was focused on the cyclorama when Simon explores the island alone and talks about the amazing sky. The use of blue to show night also symbolised the darkness that takes over the boys.

Red lights were used to create atmosphere rather than support set. The red light was used during the hunting and violent scenes. They supported the boys' aggressive gestures and scary facial expressions. The audience immediately thinks of danger when they see red and the lighting left us on the edge of our seat.

White lights were also used to create atmosphere rather than support set. The white light was used when Anthony Roberts (Piggy) was on the stage. I thought that the use of white showed the audience that Piggy was a pure character.

The first paragraph focuses on the way light is used to communicate location. There is some evaluation but you can see from the length of the paragraph that it lacks the depth and detail of a strong response.

The student is clearly at ease with terminology in the second paragraph. They show that they understand that lighting can be used to symbolise key themes. Once again there is not the depth and detail of a strong answer.

This paragraph shows that the student understand how lighting supports the choices of the performers and creates atmosphere. This is the strongest evaluation because it begins to go into more depth. It is no coincidence that this is the longest of the paragraphs.

The final paragraph is too brief to get beyond an average response but it does include analysis and evaluation.

## Overall commentary

This is an average response because:

- there is a considered selection of examples with some developed further than others
- the lack of detail and development does not allow personal conclusions to seem fully justified
- it focuses on examples on their own and doesn't make connections between them. This shows good engagement with the surface of the production.

## Student C

The colours of the lights were great. They made me pay attention to what was happening on stage. The Lord of the Flies is about a group of boys who survive a plane crash on an island with no adults. They split into groups and become more and more horrible. Two of the boys are murdered before the rest are rescued. Red light meant blood and danger. The death scenes were the best because everything got really intense. The group of boys chased one boy and kicked him to death. The acting was amazing and the fighting was really cool. A green light was used for the bits when the boys were more friendly. These bits weren't as interesting as the violence.

The thoughts are not clearly linked. There is too much retelling of the story and not enough about the performance. There is a basic understanding of what coloured lights could mean but this is not explained in enough detail. There is not enough evaluation but simple personal judgements are given instead.

## Overall commentary

This is a weak response because:

- the lack of structure does not support clear analysis
- the focus is on narrative, which shows a lack of engagement with performance and production
- evaluations are unjustified opinions and emphasise how attention was simply maintained.

# Section B : Live Theatre Evaluation

**Question 9(b)**

*Evaluate how the set was used to communicate the key ideas and themes of the performance.*  **(9 marks)**

These are sections of students' responses to show the different levels of response.

## Student A

The set for Lord of the Flies supported the theme of nightmares and hopelessness. Jon Bausor's set-design included a full-sized section of a crashed plane fuselage that filled the stage-left half of the proscenium arch space. A broken wing that created an entrance ramp for the actors was on the stage-right half. These parts of the set looked so realistic that it drew the audience into the nightmare of a plane crash. The theme of hopelessness was also communicated successfully because the boys looked so small compared to the huge crashed plane set.

> This student immediately makes the themes they are going to talk about clear. They clearly describe the details of the set and give careful reasons why it is successful at creating meaning.

Fire was used in Bausor's set design to support the ideas of survival and disaster. The boys have to light a fire to survive and decide to do it at the bottom of the wing ramp stage right. A real fire was on stage using a small, safe fire pit that was lit from below the stage floor. The position of the boys' fire at the bottom of the large broken wing emphasised how small and weak they were compared to the powerful setting. The set design allowed for the fire to appear to get out of control by spreading across a crack in the stage floor. The pyrotechnics of the set was quite shocking to watch in an indoor theatre and made me feel a real sense of danger.

> The student shows that they are aware of the way the set is an important part of the story when they describe the fire. They show an understanding of how this would have been created. The evaluative point is personal and well justified.

The set design included moving mechanical parts that bought the objects of the set to life. This supported the idea that the boys' setting was a monster. The walls of the fuselage fell away and cracks opened up in the wing ramp during the final hunting and murder scene. These set changes were remotely controlled so they seemed realistic. I could hear gasps of fear as the walls fell near the actors. The set design was the best part of the production and the audience was clearly scared of it like it was a nightmarish monster.

> The final paragraph is a strong evaluation of how mechanical movements of the set had an impact on the audience. The student makes it clear how set was used to communicate the theme of nightmares and hopelessness.

## Overall commentary

This is a strong response because:

- it is balanced and detailed with confidently-handled technical and subject-specific language
- conclusions are personal and fully justified
- the clear analysis and evaluation of challenging examples shows the student's full engagement with the production.

## Student B

The set design was impressive and realistic. When we arrived the curtain was up and we could see a crashed plane with seats falling out. Opened luggage and clothes were across the stage. The plane was the size of a real plane and this made it like we were looking in on a real world. The realistic set was quite cinematic and was great to look at. I sat waiting for the play to begin and thought about how scary it would be to be in a plane crash.

The curtain stayed up during the interval and we saw the stage hands change the set and build Ralph's shelter. Seeing this happen broke the fourth wall and made me think about why this production was being performed. The shelter was built from luggage and wreckage and was downstage centre. The central position of this part of the set clearly communicated the idea that Ralph's group was trying to be civilised.

Levels were an important part of the set design. After the interval Jack's tribe were based high up on the platform made by the tail wing of the plane. The height of this part of the set showed their power and authority over Ralph and the boys in the shelter on the lower stage floor.

The student's description is clear and they give some evaluation of the cinematic quality of the set. Unfortunately, these evaluations don't refer to the themes and ideas that the question requires.

The complex idea of breaking the fourth wall is introduced in the second paragraph with some success. There is more of a connection with demands of the question when they write about the boys trying to be civilised.

The student makes a good final point about levels but doesn't go into enough evaluative detail to back it up.

## Overall commentary

This is an average response because:

- some points are more fully analysed and evaluated than others
- there is some justification of evaluative points
- it focuses on examples on their own and doesn't make connections between them. This shows careful engagement with the surface of the production.

## Student C

The play is set on an island after a plane full of schoolboys has crashed. There are bags everywhere and the floor is sandy. I think the set looked really good. My favourite part was the inside of the plane because it looked so real. I liked the bits when the boys climbed inside. It was higher than the ground so Jack used it to show his high status. The boys decided they needed to make a fire to get the attention of passing ships. They manage to make a fire using sun light and Piggy's glasses. But the fire gets out of control and the boys have to stamp it out. This worked really well because the fire was real. Ralph and his group built a shelter out of luggage and broken aeroplane bits. It wasn't a very good shelter and was destroyed by Jack and his group. This was a horrible thing to do to Ralph. I didn't like Jack because he behaved like an animal.

The student describes the world of the play rather than the elements of the set. There is some basic awareness of how the set can symbolise themes. Evaluation is rooted in personal opinion and linked to characters and story instead of performance.

## Overall commentary

This is a weak response because:

- the lack of structure does not support clear analysis
- the focus is on the narrative world of the play, which shows a lack of engagement with performance and production
- the evaluations are unjustified opinions and only show a connection with characters.

# Drama
## Component 3: Theatre Makers in Practice

### SECTION A: BRINGING TEXTS TO LIFE
Answer ALL questions that relate to the ONE performance text studied for examination purposes. There are five questions in total for each performance text.

*1984*, George Orwell, by Robert Icke and Duncan Macmillan

**Answer ALL questions.**

**You are involved in staging a production of this play. Please read the extract on pages 56–59 from** *'Then-then Goldstein is a real person'* **to** *'I know how it ends'*

1. (a) There are specific choices in this extract for performers.

   (i) You are going to play Winston. Explain **two** ways you would use **vocal skills** to play this character in this extract. **(4)**

   (ii) You are going to play O'Brien. He has the highest status in this extract. As a performer, give **three** suggestions of how you would use **performance skills** to show his power and authority in this extract.
   You must provide a reason for each suggestion. **(6)**

   (b) There are specific choices in this extract for a director.

   (i) As a director, discuss how you would use **one** of the **production elements below** to bring this extract to life for your audience.
   You should make reference to the context in which the text was created and performed.

   Choose **one** of the following:
   - costume
   - staging
   - props/stage furniture. **(9)**

   (ii) Julia has a significant role in the play as a whole but she speaks very little in this extract.
   As a director, discuss how the performer might play the role in this extract and the complete play.
   You must consider:
   - voice
   - physicality
   - stage directions and stage space. **(12)**

   (c) There are specific choices in this extract for designers.

   Discuss how you would use **one** design element to enhance the production of this extract for the audience.
   Choose **one** of the following:
   - set
   - lighting
   - sound. **(14)**

**Total for Question 1 = 45 marks**
**TOTAL FOR SECTION A = 45 MARKS**

*An Inspector Calls* **by J.B Priestley**

**Answer ALL questions.**

**You are involved in staging a production of this play. Please read the extract in Act 2 pages 46–49 from Mrs Birling:** *'Oh, stop it, both of you'* **to the end of the Act.**

2. (a) There are specific choices in this extract for performers.

(i) You are going to play Sheila. Explain **two** ways you would use **physical skills** to play this character in this extract. **(4)**

(ii) You are going to play Inspector Goole. He is in control of the questioning and therefore very important in this scene.
As a performer, give **three** suggestions of how you would use **performance skills** to show his importance in this extract.
You must provide a reason for each suggestion. **(6)**

(b) There are specific choices in this extract for a director.

(i) As a director, discuss how you would use **one** of the **production elements below** to bring this extract to life for your audience.
You should make reference to the context in which the text was created and performed.

Choose **one** of the following:
• costume
• staging
• props/stage furniture. **(9)**

(ii) The Inspector interrogates Mrs Birling in this extract: she resents the Inspector's intrusion and feels that her actions were entirely justified.
As a director, discuss how the performer playing this role might demonstrate her attitude to the audience in this extract and the complete play.
You must consider:
• voice
• physicality
• stage directions and stage space. **(12)**

(c) There are specific choices in this extract for designers.

Discuss how you would use **one** design element to enhance the production of this extract for the audience.
Choose **one** of the following:
• set
• lighting
• sound. **(14)**

**Total for Question 2 = 45 marks**
**TOTAL FOR SECTION A = 45 MARKS**

*Blue Stockings* **by Jessica Swale**

**Answer ALL questions.**

**You are involved in staging a production of this play. Act 1 Scene 4, pages 31–33 from** '*Let's abandon the fanciful speculation*' **to the end of the scene.**

3. (a) There are specific choices in this extract for performers.

    (i) You are going to play Lloyd. Explain **two** ways you would use **vocal skills** to play this character in this extract. **(4)**

    (ii) You are going to play Tess. She is humiliated in this scene because she has the confidence to challenge Dr Maudsley's theories.
As a performer, give **three** suggestions of how you would use **performance skills** to show this in the extract. You must provide a reason for each suggestion. **(6)**

  (b) There are specific choices in this extract for a director.

    (i) As a director, discuss how you would use **one** of the **production elements below** to bring this extract to life for your audience.
You should make reference to the context in which the text was created and performed.

    Choose **one** of the following:
- costume
- staging
- props/stage furniture. **(9)**

    (ii) Dr Maudsley belittles Tess because she is a woman who dares to challenge his theories. As a director, discuss how the performer playing this role might demonstrate this attitude to the audience in this extract and the complete play.
You must consider:

- voice
- physicality
- stage directions and stage space. **(12)**

  (c) There are specific choices in this extract for designers.

    Discuss how you would use **one** design element to enhance the production of this extract for the audience. Choose **one** of the following:
- set
- lighting
- sound. **(14)**

**Total for Question 3 = 45 marks**
**TOTAL FOR SECTION A = 45 MARKS**

## The Crucible by Arthur Miller

### Answer ALL questions.

**You are involved in staging a production of this play. Please read the extract in Act 3 pages 103–106 from '...*this girl has always struck me false*' to '*GIRLS* raising their fists *Stop it!!*'**

4. (a) There are specific choices in this extract for performers.

(i) You are going to play Danforth. Explain **two** ways you would use **vocal skills** to play this character in this extract.  **(4)**

(ii) You are going to play Mary Warren. In this scene Abigail and the girls accuse her of witchcraft. As a performer, give **three** suggestions of how you would use **performance skills** to show her fear in the extract. You must provide a reason for each suggestion.  **(6)**

(b) There are specific choices in this extract for a director.

(i) As a director, discuss how you would use **one** of the **production elements below** to bring this extract to life for your audience.
You should make reference to the context in which the text was created and performed.

Choose **one** of the following:
- costume
- staging
- props/stage furniture.  **(9)**

(ii) Abigail leads the other girls in pretending that Mary Warren is bewitching them. As a director, discuss how the performer playing this role might demonstrate Abigail's dominance to the audience in this extract and the complete play.
You must consider:

- voice
- physicality
- stage directions and stage space.  **(12)**

(c) There are specific choices in this extract for designers.

Discuss how you would use **one** design element to enhance the production of this extract for the audience.
Choose **one** of the following:
- set
- lighting
- sound.  **(14)**

**Total for Question 4 = 45 marks**
**TOTAL FOR SECTION A = 45 MARKS**

*DNA* by Dennis Kelly

**Answer ALL questions.**

**You are involved in staging a production of this play. Please read the extract in Scene 3 pages 49–52 where Adam appears from** *'They stand around a boy who looks like a tramp'* **to** *'Say something Phil,* Pause. But Phil says nothing'

5  (a) There are specific choices in this extract for performers.

   (i) You are going to play Cathy. Explain **two** ways you would use **vocal skills** to play this character in
      this extract.                                                                                    **(4)**

   (ii) You are going to play Adam. He has been living in the woods and is disorientated and afraid. As a performer,
      give **three** suggestions of how you would use **performance skills** to show his confusion in the extract.
      You must provide a reason for each suggestion.                                                   **(6)**

   (b) There are specific choices in this extract for a director.

   (i) As a director, discuss how you would use **one** of the **production elements below** to bring this extract to life for
      your audience.
      You should make reference to the context in which the text was created and performed.

      Choose **one** of the following:
      • costume
      • staging
      • props/stage furniture.                                                                         **(9)**

   (ii) Brian has been affected by the pressure and become unbalanced. As a director, discuss how the performer
      playing this role might demonstrate Brian's mental state to the audience in this extract and the complete play.
      You must consider:

      • voice
      • physicality
      • stage directions and stage space.                                                              **(12)**

   (c) There are specific choices in this extract for designers.

      Discuss how you would use **one** design element to enhance the production of this extract for the audience.
      Choose **one** of the following:
      • set
      • lighting
      • sound.                                                                                          **(14)**

**Total for Question 5 = 45 marks**
**TOTAL FOR SECTION A = 45 MARKS**

## Dr Korczak's Example by David Grieg

### Answer ALL questions.

**You are involved in staging a production of this play. Please read Scene 18 pages 54–56.**

6. (a) There are specific choices in this extract for performers.

(i) You are going to play The Priest. Explain **two** ways you would use **vocal skills** to play this character in this extract. **(4)**

(ii) You are going to play Stephanie. She allows herself to be influenced by Adzio in this scene give **three** suggestions of how you would use **performance skills** to show her change of attitude in this extract. You must provide a reason for each suggestion. **(6)**

(b) There are specific choices in this extract for a director.

(i) As a director, discuss how you would use **one** of the **production elements below** to bring this extract to life for your audience.
You should make reference to the context in which the text was created and performed.

Choose **one** of the following:
- costume
- staging
- props/stage furniture. **(9)**

(ii) Adzio is an angry character and in this scene he demonstrates his frustration
As a director, discuss how the performer playing this role might show his anger in this extract and the complete play.
You must consider:
- voice
- physicality
- stage directions and stage space. **(12)**

(c) There are specific choices in this extract for designers.

Discuss how you would use **one** design element to enhance the production of this extract for the audience.
Choose **one** of the following:
- set
- lighting
- sound. **(14)**

**Total for Question 6 = 45 marks**
**TOTAL FOR SECTION A = 45 MARKS**

*Government Inspector* **by Nickoli Gogol in a version by David Harrower**

**Answer ALL questions.**

**You are involved in staging a production of this play. Please read the extract in Act 2 Scene 4 pages 42–45 from** *'I'll take it'* **to the end of the act.**

7. (a) There are specific choices in this extract for performers.

   (i) You are going to play Bobchinsky. Explain **two** ways you would use **physical skills** to play this character
      in this extract. **(4)**

   (ii) You are going to play Khlestakov. He is enjoying his high status in this scene. As a performer, give **three**
       suggestions of how you would use **performance skills** to show this in the extract.
       You must provide a reason for each suggestion. **(6)**

  (b) There are specific choices in this extract for a director.

   (i) As a director, discuss how you would use **one** of the **production elements below** to bring this extract to life for
      your audience.
      You should make reference to the context in which the text was created and performed.

      Choose **one** of the following:
      • costume
      • staging
      • props/stage furniture. **(9)**

   (ii) The Mayor persuades Khlestakov to stay at his house so that he can influence his opinion of the town. As
      a director, discuss how the performer playing this role might demonstrate the Mayor's efforts to impress
      Khlestakov to the audience in this extract and the complete play.
      You must consider:

      • voice
      • physicality
      • stage directions and stage space. **(12)**

  (c) There are specific choices in this extract for designers.

      Discuss how you would use **one** design element to enhance the production of this extract for the audience.
      Choose **one** of the following:
      • set
      • lighting
      • sound. **(14)**

**Total for Question 7 = 45 marks**
**TOTAL FOR SECTION A = 45 MARKS**

### Twelfth Night by William Shakespeare

**Answer ALL questions.**

**You are involved in staging a production of this play. Please read the extract in Act 2 Scene 5 lines 80–180** *'What employment have we here'* **to** *'Exit'*

8. (a) There are specific choices in this extract for performers.

  (i) You are going to play Fabian. Explain **two** ways you would use **vocal skills** to play this character in this extract.

  **(4)**

  (ii) You are going to play Sir Toby Belch. He is higher status than Malvolio and was involved in tricking him with the forged letter. As a performer, give **three** suggestions of how you would use **performance skills** to show Sir Toby's enjoyment of the plan's success in this extract.
  You must provide a reason for each suggestion.

  **(6)**

  (b) There are specific choices in this extract for a director.

  (i) As a director, discuss how you would use **one** of the **production elements below** to bring this extract to life for your audience.
  You should make reference to the context in which the text was created and performed.

  Choose **one** of the following:
  - costume
  - staging
  - props/stage furniture.

  **(9)**

  (ii) Malvolio is an important comic character in the play. As a director, discuss how the performer playing this role might play the role in this extract and the complete play.
  You must consider:

  - voice
  - physicality
  - stage directions and stage space.

  **(12)**

  (c) There are specific choices in this extract for designers.

  Discuss how you would use **one** design element to enhance the production of this extract for the audience.
  Choose **one** of the following:
  - set
  - lighting
  - sound.

  **(14)**

**Total for Question 8 = 45 marks**
**TOTAL FOR SECTION A = 45 MARKS**

**SECTION B: LIVE THEATRE EVALUATION**

**Answer both questions on the performance you have seen.**

9. (a) Analyse how the actors' movement was used to engage the audience during one key moment of the performance.

(6)

(b) Evaluate how the set was used to communicate the key themes and ideas of the performance.

(9)